UNConventional
Wisdom

*UN*Conventional Wisdom

METHODS OF BEHAVIOR MODIFICATION FOR THE MODERN AGE

R.C. Seely

Sermo datur cunctis; animi sapientia paucis.

Introduction **TO PAVLOVISM**

Brainwashing by the political elite is not a new concept; in fact across the globe it's extremely common. In the first chapter I am going to present the ways in which we are held in the control of the collective culture. The foundation for the rest of this book is the principles in this chapter.

It also introduces the readers to the author and what I do under my blog Americanus Libertae.

WHAT IS CONVENTIONAL WISDOM?

Conventional Wisdom, in its most basic and simple definitions, is the end results of the colluded efforts by the elites in society to create a perceived version of realty. In this effort the list of perpetrators is many and varied: the media, big business, the government, and at times by society itself, in the form of conspiracy theorists. The tools used by these in cooperation is as varied as the perpetrators and includes, propaganda, censorship, group think, party line thinking and pop culture manipulation, are just a few examples of this.

So what is the fundamental cause of all this? Federalism. Federalism is the philosophy that a strong central government should be established to protect the people, even from themselves. Supposedly it should act as a pillar for society, holding up the weight of a civil and just culture. In realty the weight is in fact on top of the people suffocating the citizenry with its inflexibility and false promises.

Under federalism, we should build a wall and got involved other nation's affairs to either help build them up or tear them down. Instead both actions have backfired, the wall penning us in like livestock and our actions abroad have kept us in a perpetual State of emergency in the process; making more enemies with our intrusions and putting the United States in more danger.

Federalist Alexander Hamilton kept pushing and pushing for a federal bank to protect our financial interests. It became a behemoth that fostered cronyism and had to be torn down. Federalism has been tried and failed. Those who were charged with the duty of protecting the people have instead enslaved them. They make claims that their policies are safety nets meant to improve our lives and make us more free, but those ideas have turned on the people and are now smothering them into submission.

Even more, those in power keep granting themselves more control by taking the rights that are the states and claiming them as their own. The war on drugs, economic issues, immigration, marriage rights, abortion and education; all are issues that should be and can be managed by the states. Historically, far better too, since the states have constraints that are more easily enforced and they have to be beholden to budget and their constituency. That's what I'm going to be covering in this book, making observations and bringing points that most don't consider and asking the questions most don't ask. In the last chapter there are a list of conclusions and solutions to these problems. If you can learn to do this, you too might be able to see the *Unconventional Wisdom* in everyday life.

Inside Americanus Libertae

In 2012 I started the *Americanus Libertae* movement with the agenda of fighting the wide-spread myths within our popular culture, but in the end it had changed to mostly advancing the third party options.

While researching for my blog, I came across interesting information that has made me reevaluate my original preconceived notions. Some have been slightly tweaked, others have completely changed. What I discovered about Unconventional Wisdom is that the best way to be prepared to see it is to keep an open mind but stay skeptical.

Now that might sound like a contradiction, but it is actually a very rational and organized way of thinking once you're used to it.

That's the goal of this book, mental reconditioning to get the reader used to questioning everything but still not dismissing all the possibilities. Understanding without fully believing, complex thinking about the most simple of truths. In the end it is important to remember this is subjective analysis, this is not a presentation of an investigator, but by a social commentator. This is not absolute fact, but learning to question absolute facts. I encourage others to question my findings and create an open dialogue with your peers.

That's what the *Americanus Libertae* movement has always been about, a voice of the people by a blue collar American. Finding out what the people think and a discussion with ordinary citizens, not political science specialists. This is by far more important than trying to convince anyone that I'm right and that's all. Teaching others *how* to think rather than *what* to think.

Pavlovian Social Engineering

In an issue of *First Freedom* magazine, there were articles about comments that Eric Holder and Michael Bloomberg said - about their agenda to brainwash the people into adopting the attitude that guns are wrong. Brainwashing! Really? So rather than trying to even attempt to have a reasonable discussion with the citizens, they are going to try *force* to get them to give up their guns. Wow!

What these tools are not even considering in their equation - Most who keep guns don't buy into the propaganda and they are not going to just turn in their guns. The government will have to go in and take them, so their plan won't be a nice and easy walk in the park. That's the good news, the bad news there are some small victories on their side. When you read posts on twitter, face book, you tube or other social media sites, the sad truth is the anti-gun crowd has had minor success - far too many are regurgitating the same lies of politicians like Bloomberg. This is a prime example of what I call - *Pavlovain Social Engineering.*

For those unfamiliar with Pavlov and his experiments, his study was on mental conditioning.

In his most famous experiment on conditioning was when he got his dogs to drool with the sound of a bell. He reasoned that salivating is an unconditioned response done unconsciously and did it automatically when food was presented - but could it be a conditioned response? Apparently so. In his

4

experiments when he would feed the dogs he would also ring a bell. He continued this for a while - ringing the bell when feeding them - until one day he just rang the bell, without the food. The dogs started drooling at the sound of the bell, because it is associated with food.

Anyone who has kept other animals could testify that animals will greet their owners when they have food. Pet snakes are placed in a separate cage for feeding, because it will associate the opening of the cage with food and if fed in their regular cage might bite the owner. I've even seen a lizard do this once by simply opening the cage it started twitching its tail, like it does when it's ready to strike at prey.

The Three Absolutes

Most people use one of three absolute rationales to decide how they want policy made. The first two sound good and benevolent, but they are loaded with bias and are unfair to someone.

We have Virtuous Absolutism, Emotional Absolutism and Ethical (or Legal) Absolutism.

Virtuous Absolutism is a philosophy that policies need be to set by a dogmatic or theological basis. Why is this wrong? Because you're imprinting your own principles on others, this always eliminates choice and accountability. Worse still it gives the interpretive power of your personal beliefs to the government. Usually this is used by the Republican Party.

Emotional Absolutism is a philosophy that policies need be in line with the tenets of manufactured equality. This isn't right either, because it gives too much power not only to the government, but also lobbyists and union leaders - it typically leads to cronyism. Usually used by the Democratic Party.

Ethical Absolutism is the philosophy that we need to strictly adhere to legal statutes and constitutional principles. No hyperbole. No special interests. No artificial equality. No tyranny. Simply free choice.

The Absolutes in Action

Now that I have explained the existence of these absolutes, let's go into an example of these absolutes being used.

Take these unfortunate domestic terrorist acts of school shootings. When one of these incidents occur, the bias absolutes are clear and usually follow party lines. Republicans claim that it is the fault of the violence in video games, books and other media. But the evidence for this is scant. Mostly it's a subjective opinion by pundits who already are against video games, seeing them as a waste of time or having no redeemable value. Reality shows have no redeemable value, but blaming them for moral degradation doesn't get much traction.

The only more absurd argument is from the other side. Getting guns from the people will make them safer? How does that work? The open gun laws are a balance of power, everything is about checks and balances, so should guns. But keep in mind the second amendment is not about gun rights, it's about the right of self-preservation.

At least the gun grabbers are clear with their intensions (warped as they may be); the same can't be said from the other extreme. Is the game-plan from that side simply informing the parents? Or are they suggesting a more *hands on* approach? If disclosure is their plan that's fine, but if the agenda is one of censorship an actual study needs to be done - by impartial researchers.

Here's my analysis of this.

First, there were signs. These were not unpredictable tragedies that could not have been avoided. The gun laws worked, it was family intervention that got the firearm in their hands.

Hours and hours of violent media and games is not the cause, it's a *symptom* of the underlying problem. This is violence addiction, the cruel primordial, tribal part of our individual biological makeup. A lot of us have a small percentage of this. That's why destruction therapy works. For those who don't know what this is, it's a psychological treatment where you take a club to a donated vehicle. The games do have a positive function as it is another form of this therapy. Monitor the amount of time that the children spend on the games, but let them participate in that weekend HALO tournament.

The solutions to this problem are not as clear as the ignored signs. Part of the problem is that as far as we have come with dismantling other archaic perspectives, one that continues to flourish is the stigmas connected to seeking help with mental health issues. The two boys who committed the Columbine massacre, for example had a history of violence. The shooter at Aurora, CO also had a history of mental issues prior to the shooting. They also have been described as quiet loners who are extremely smart.

Another phenomenon is that after the initial incident, there is a rash of additional shootings, and then they stop. What causes this? The media attention emboldens others to act. Which begs the question - What function (if any) does a lack of attention and affection play in this? Charles Manson didn't know parental love. Neither did Jeffery Dahmer. Could that be what is causing this? A home devoid of attention? Studies have shown that babies deprived of attention have suffered debilitating health issues. Those in the studies also have similar anti-social tendencies, as those who commit these acts of violence.

I'm not saying this should excuse them from prosecution for their crimes by any means. Keeping an eye out for the traits mentioned are preventative, not as validation for them. In the end; violence in the media, over coverage by the media, lack of gun laws all have the unintended consequence of taking the responsibility off the perpetrators; and runs the risks of over eager legislatures decreeing security over liberty. If the solutions proposed require giving one of our rights, then is it worth it? Once you open *Pandora's Box*, can we close it again?

Not a Justification, but an Explanation

Just to be clear about this, I'm not saying that violence addiction (or any addiction) is a valid excuse for breaking the law. Many people have had an abusive childhood and turned out fine, many others have overcome such adversities.

Take the Aria Castro case, this sick and demented sociopath abducts, rapes, and holds hostage, three young women from his neighborhood. What was his excuse? An abusive childhood, can't you be a little more original than that! How long is that old narrative going to be abused? He got a bad hand, that sucks, but that doesn't excuse the violation of other people's rights, let only their physical bodies.

The argument by anti-death penalty groups is that since these monsters - the ones who have destroyed the lives of innocent people - should receive a pass because of their destructive childhood. Advocating for the victim, that's supposed to be the democrat's platform right, what about those hurt by these emotionless men and women? Who's their advocate? If a killer or rapist is given only a slap on the wrist, how does the justice system achieve justice? Who gets justice in this way? - It's certainly not the victim! Or their families.

But I don't think even the perpetrators do. They still have to suffer with their compulsion they can't control. This is not like, smoking, gambling or realty show addiction; it can't be solved with treatment. They have violated others and have lost the privilege of being a part of a civil society. That is why they should get the death penalty, closure for themselves and their victims.

There is validity in the arguments that since innocent people get put in jail and do end up on death row, so the death penalty should be abolished. Now I respect the stance that it is better that 100 guilty go free than one innocent be put to death... I just don't agree with it. There will unfortunately be innocent people that end up getting the death penalty, that's the cost of setting up an imperfect system by flawed beings, but if one serial killer is set free there could be as many or even more to die at their hands.

The death penalty does work; it's in the enforcement of the law that at times falters. Innocent people are on death row because of overzealous representatives of the law, that's the part that needs to be reviewed and improved on. Coddling these deviants, empowers them, turning the general public into insects about to get their wings or legs pulled off.

The Obama Youth

One of the keys to capturing control of a nation by an ambitious leader is to control its education system. Common Core is part of this - common core is an extremist education, advancing the progressive social justice ideology to American children. Mixed into the reading list, of such classics like: *To Kill a Mockingbird, Alice's Adventures in Wonderland,* Voltaire's *Candide* and *Metamorphosis* by Kafka, and writings by Thomas Jefferson, Abraham Lincoln and Thomas Paine; are controversial books by contemporary authors with divisive agendas. Included in the list of authors are members of the Sierra Club and other activists groups and not the input of the parents. When the validity of the books being on a list of recommended reading for a school is brought up by a parent; such as the book *Invisible Man* by Ralph Ellison, which is sexually explicit in nature, was requested to be removed by a parent in North Carolina she was ignored; or the book *Dreaming in Cuba* by Cristina Garcia, which has the following sexually explicit scene:

"Hugo and Felicia stripped in their room dissolving into one another... Hugo bit Felicia's breast and purplish... bruises on her upper thighs. He knelt before her in the tub and massaged[her]... soap between her legs, He entered her repeatedly from behind.

"Felicia learned what pleased him. She tied his arms above his head with their underclothing and slapping him sharply when he asked.

" 'You're my bitch,' Hugo said, groaning.

"In the morning he left, promising to return in the summer."

Oh isn't that sweet that your children are being taught the finer points of the *S and M* culture in school? The parts of the curriculum that are valid and "historically" accurate texts are about as historically accurate in their portait of history, as reality shows are of real life. In one section the author makes the absurd assertion the Native Americans were strictly hunters and didn't do any farming, claiming in this way they were a more "affluent" people because they weren't burdened by materialism - this is a blatant case of anti-capitalism. One of the books *If the World was a Village* is an introduction to the theory of overpopulation and another *Words we Live By: Your Anointed Guide to the Constitution,* encourages racial division and feminism, and ignores how much harm it has done. *Save Lord God Bird,* instructs on saving animals from extinction. One of the most apparent examples of indoctrination is in one lesson the US EPA/US Department of Energy's, *Recommended Levels of Insulation* report, now that will keep the kids awake.

All that common core is, is a typical government program, taught not to question, which includes in one of the lessons a quote from Franklin Roosevelt (it wouldn't be complete without it!):

Roosevelt, Franklin Delano. "State of the Union Address." (1941)

"For there is nothing mysterious about the foundations of a healthy and strong democracy. The basic things expected by our people of their political and economic systems are simple. They are:

Equality of opportunity for youth and for others.

Jobs for those who can work.

Security for those who need it.

The ending of special privilege for the few.

The preservation of civil liberties for all.

The enjoyment of the fruits of scientific progress in a wider and constantly rising standard of living.

These are the simple, basic things that must never be lost sight of in the turmoil and unbelievable complexity of our modern world. The inner and abiding strength of our economic and political systems is dependent upon the degree to which they fulfill these expectations. Many subjects connected with our social economy call for immediate improvement.
As examples:

We should bring more citizens under the coverage of old-age pensions and unemployment insurance.

We should widen the opportunities for adequate medical care.

We should plan a better system by which persons deserving or needing gainful employment may obtain it.

I have called for personal sacrifice. I am assured of the willingness of almost all Americans to respond to that call.
A part of the sacrifice means the payment of more money in taxes. In my Budget Message I shall recommend that a greater portion of this great defense program be paid for from taxation than we are paying today. No person should try, or be allowed, to get rich out of this program; and the

principle of tax payments in accordance with ability to pay should be constantly before our eyes to guide our legislation.

If the Congress maintains these principles, the voters, putting patriotism ahead of pocketbooks, will give you their applause.

In the future days, which we seek to make secure, we look forward to a world founded upon four essential human freedoms.

The first is freedom of speech and expression—everywhere in the world.

The second is freedom of every person to worship God in his own way—everywhere in the world.

The third is freedom from want—which, translated into world terms, means economic understandings which will secure to every nation a healthy peacetime life for its inhabitants-everywhere in the world.

The fourth is freedom from fear—which, translated into world terms, means a world-wide reduction of armaments to such a point and in such a thorough fashion that no nation will be in a position to commit an act of physical aggression against any neighbor—anywhere in the world."

Of course they make it sound sooo appealing. For more on the curriculum of Common Core, go to *corestandards.org*, that's the source for this segment.

If all this weren't bad enough, the children are being indoctrinated into - *Obamaism*. A school of thought that Obama is the greatest, that he is never wrong, that he is God incarnated. Insert vomit here!

Obama from what I've seen has not been right on much of anything. Even on social issues he hasn't been right! He has to get involved in everything - expand the government - rather than letting the states set their own policies according to their individual needs.

As for the tactics of the Obama education system, it looks a little too similar to the Hitler youth program - let's put the man before the nation.

Freedom Over Free stuff

Obama-phones, expanded welfare, planned parenthood, are just a few of the government bribes we call: Entitlements. When asked on the radio interview about where Obama where he would get the money to fulfill his vast promises the predictable response was essentially - don't know, don't care. Many are under the conclusion that these things are really "free stuff." For some in our country that is the case, but if you pay taxes, you're paying for it and so is every other taxpayer. This is where the anger of many (myself included) lies.

All these social programs should not be subsidized - because of the lack of efficiency and accountability - no program has been run as well or with less waste as the government program versus the privatized version of it. All the current fiscal problems are due to this lack of restraint and it stems from having no respect for the taxpayers money, or that they have a right to know and decide where that money goes.

Cheap means Inferior

This is a lesson that is very hard to learn, I had to learn it through trial and error. A few years ago I was looking for a replacement car, since mine was getting up there in both years and miles and was starting to have issues. So I went around town looking at the different car lots, after a series of aggressive salesmen I found a low-key one that treated me with respect. I ended up buying one from that dealership; part of the reason was because the salesman wasn't trying to hustle me, but the other was I didn't fully explore my options.

See I could have utilized a contact I had at one of the dealerships and gotten the same car for less. But that didn't even occur to me; what did matter was that getting the same car for less was for some reason … unsettling, maybe even unnatural. That's because conventional thinking has modeled our first intention to distrust those offering the better deal. If it's so much less, what's wrong with it? It's good to be suspicious of deals that sound too good, but we should also be skeptical of those asking the higher price. Because sometimes the better price is just that, the better price.

At times the trade-offs are not important to us. We sacrifice options that don't matter - heated seats in a dry, hot climate for most of the year, a simpler stereo system, plain wheels, for a few examples. Dealers will also sell products and services for a lot less, knowing that there will be enough patrons to offset the lower markup. At times cheap and inexpensive are two completely different things and in this case I missed out on a good deal because of it. Oh well, live and learn.

Payment Over Principle

If you watch the news you can tell the difference between those who are passionate about an issue and those who have been coerced into attendance. Those who are at an event to protest who care are far more angry, more engaged, and in larger numbers.

At the staged protests the protesters are in the thousands at best, but at the legitimate protests however the numbers are in the hundreds of thousands.

So how do we end up with even that many who don't care? Many are bored, others are joining the bandwagon, and those trying to get into in office do so to gain political points. The worst though, are the group not talked about much - the paid protester. I hate paid protesters! Their existence makes things more convoluted by giving the illusion that the issue has more public support than it has.

17

All Dietary Needs are the Same

One of the most prevailing social myths is that of dietary needs. For years the conventional wisdom has been that salt and sugars are bad for us and that wisdom has been unchallenged truth for a long time.

But in this era of skepticism that wisdom has finally been properly examined and research has shown that it's a relatively small portion of the populace that would have serious health complications from exceeding the original recommended doses of either salt or sugar. In fact, studies have shown the opposite is true and most of us are *deficient* in one or both of these minerals. Same as gluten, in modern times, the fact is gluten is an excellent source of protein and should only be avoided if you have an allergy to it or other health conditions acerbated by it. If you don't have to avoid it, then feel good about enjoying it!

Chapter **ONE**

<u>ARE YOU HAPPY?</u>

When I first began working on this book, this was my first idea. Simply covering how censorship and propaganda affects our emotional and psychological state. As with most of my writing projects what started out as a small single encompassing concept. But as I started pondering this I realized that this was one minute part of a larger problem.

Beating the Hype

Censorship is the cornerstone of propaganda and the control of information the general public does or doesn't have access to without it the path to creating reality for the masses would fall apart. That is why so many of the information generators of the monopoly media eagerly advance the tenets of the popular culture movement. Pop culture encourages the masses what to think not how to think and that's why I despise them!

The prime directive here is that no crisis be wasted, that actually was what Rahm Emanuel said verbatim in a press statement, also saying it is, *"an opportunity for us to do things that you could not do before."* Maybe there's a reason we didn't "do things that you could not do before!"

That's hype and it can be a very effective way to rally the public to a cause, but it is very manipulative. With emotional manipulation the general public will give up their rights and even go against their own best interests. Hype could be considered a form of censorship because the truth is hidden from the public - this is censorship by omission.

What's interesting is those who call for an end to censorship by omission are the ones most guilty of it. That's why the *Fairness Doctrine* and the *FCC* were really invented for.

Think an issue might have hype added to it? Read the phrasing carefully and watch for emotional arguments, if the emotional arguments aren't backed up by any logical weight or facts, be wary. Find out more information about the issue and the authors to see if they have any biases. The truth lies between the emotional lines.

Once you can see the issue without all the emotion it's easier to say no to the bad laws. Without the emotion you can go for our own best interests and still feel good about it.

Too Many Choices, My Head Hurts

"I hate going shopping, there too many different options." This is a complaint I've heard a lot and it has always baffled me. Too many choices? Is that a real complaint? If you really think about it, it's an odd complaint. I've always loved how many choices we have. It's awesome!

If I don't want plain M&M's, there are about five different flavors year round, during the holidays it increases to about twelve!

Growing up I used to hate Pringles potato chips - it came in one flavor and it was like eating paper. Bland and flavorless! Now look at the different flavors. It all came about because the number of snack food companies making chips has increased and somewhere, someone in the company that makes Pringles knew it was to their advantage to offer more choices. Actually it was more than that and about the company's very survival - adapt or die! So they did.

If history has taught us nothing else, then we

should take this lesson to heart - the free market fosters progress, variety and efficiency; the government will hinder progress, variety and create waste.

When the telephone was introduced to the public and the government had its hands in that market; we had one company AT&T, no options in services or products and questionable quality of service. After those regulations were lifted, the floodgates of innovation spewed a tidal wave of eager competition to topple the telephone monopoly and making the technology we have today.

The establishment of the *FCC* is another clear sign that more choice less government makes a product greatly improved and more desired. The presented rationale for the FCC was a need for fairness, but it was really instituted to censor opposing opinion. After the *fairness doctrine* (the FCC primary platform legislature) was repealed, interest in the radio increased.

So what does this have to do with the present? Well, they have made somewhat of a re-emergence. Bills have been coming up calling for censorship of the internet and reinstituting the fairness doctrine have also been suggested. The need for unfettered information is too important to put in the hands of government, state or federal. If we start forfeiting our choices when does it end?

So, whether it is potato chips, the telephone, radio, television, the internet, or any product or service really, having more choices is good and a sign of a thriving and needed market. Rather than quibble about the temporary inconvenience, we should praise that we have the ability to pursue and invent such variety.

P.C.: Peoples Censorship

What good does political correctness do? Its proponents say that it's to be "culturally sensitive", but there are so many examples of minorities and women that have used Political Correct to censor opinions they disagree with.

We even have laws to protect both demographics that serve only to give them an unequal balance in their opinions - eliminating equality. How can you have equality if it's manufactured?

That's only part of the flaws in Politically Correct speech; with this form of censorship we also miss out on the possibility of finding reasonable egalitarian solutions to the issues in question - all so that we don't offend someone's individual sensibilities. Grow up people! You will have to deal with those that will say stupid and insensitive things, because they are obsessed with the superficial interior doesn't give you the right to deny their rights to express themselves, no matter how absurd what they have to say or in extreme causes sue them because of it.

All that this Political Correctness movement does is create a culture where we are afraid to speak our minds and are fixated on not offending others rather than focusing on the merits of the arguments.

The nation has gone from a culture of free speech into one of free speech, with exceptions.

Gm Foods: Surge or Saving Grace

We all have heard the horror stories of the GM (Genetically Modified) foods in the news. How supposedly, it's an industry that destroys the environment and places profit over people. I too fell for the propaganda. The evidence says something completely different though. That is another case of setting convention over spreading Wisdom.

One of the early manipulation techniques outlawed before it could be properly studied and understood, is the Practice of radiating foods to make them save to eat. The logical conclusion to this is fairly obvious. Radiated Foods? We can't eat that, or we will certainly end up with a society of mutants. The reality is there is no evidence of this. The absorption rate of our crops is practically non-existent, with concern to radiation. Even with Chemicals it's extremely low. That's why the dangers of pesticides on our crops are a logical fallacy.

Not only are the damages greatly exaggerated, the benefits are downplayed. The most mentioned concerns in this subject are the increase of allergens in food from the manipulation of the crops makeup. Actually, empirical evidence points the other way, to a decrease in allergens. By altering the parts of the plant responsible for these reactions, the effects can

23

be discarded or at least lessened.

After that come the concerns about pesticides, with both increased amounts and threat of cross-contamination. Both dangers here it seems have been exaggerated as well. Studies by the National Center for Food and Agricultural Policy, have noted a substantial increase in crop yields, with a simultaneous decrease of 776,000 pounds annual usage of pesticides.

This is not limited to only the United States. Use of these biotech crops are being used across the globe, especially in developed countries with similar results. In China, for example cotton workers pesticide poisoning numbers have dropped by 75%.

As for cross contamination, this is a much hyped up concern. Buffers have been in place to make sure this doesn't happen. While it can't be 100% contained, it is for the most part an anomaly.

Fact is that policies are in place to minimize the accidental breeding of "super-weeds."

Citizens of many countries *want* to participate in the GM Food Market. Why? These foods are just poison aren't they? Only their governments seem to think so, the people say they are willing to take the risks. In the fight to end world hunger GM foods looks to be an "Atomic Bomb" ending famine across the planet. With the manipulation of the crops, food that could be grown only in tropical regions or in areas with nutrient rich soil can be plentiful in arid deserts or areas of high acidity or alkalinity. The only real impediment to all this is the government.

Even the detractors say that the fear mongering is more about "possibilities" and not proven scenarios. No confirmed cases of harm have been proven, simply speculated. Without seeing the parameters of the tests, even the famous *Monsanto* conspiracy should be viewed with skepticism, considering the attitudes of antagonism by the organic farmers.

The evidence shows more that this is more about the organic farmers trying to create a monopoly, by edging out the GM Food Market. The GM market does not share this attitude and many farmers grow both kinds of crops.

In short, it appears that the only people not happy with this invasion are those afraid of the competition or have an agenda to control the masses. The GM foods industry proves to be a risk worth taking. It's also being monitored by many different agencies including; the EPA, FDA, USDA, French Academics of Medicine and Science, FAO, the World Health Organization, the UK's Royal Society and the AMA, among others.

So it seems that the conventional wisdom says press on, while the conventional hype says reign in. One more time when propaganda has a lead over truth - does that make you happy?

Too High a Cost to Bear

When talk comes up about enforcing a new proposed legislature, the common argument against it is always the cost. Some think this is distasteful, but obviously they have more money than the general public, or they have the general public's money.

If the laws to label foods GMO or non-GMO were to get passed, we would see a massive increase in the costs at the supermarket. This would be unfortunate for those of us who are fine with ingesting GMO products and can't afford their organic counterparts. So, why the increase in costs?

First of all, a regulatory commission would need to be established, to come up with the new legal guide lines and regulations.

Then, they need to research every store that sells food. The only way to make sure the guide lines are being followed is with a food Gestapo, hiring many *more* government employees.

That's not even including the already high costs and fees associated with producing GMO foods. Or the increase that the general public will have to absorb in new costs because of marketing and research and packaging development, to be applied to non-GMO foods.

Lastly, there would be a high bill for the cost of recalling the non-GMO products.

All these new fees and registrations would be passed to both consumers, not only those who have a preference for only organic foods. If people want their food labeled non-GMO, it's a financial burden that should be placed on *them*, **not** *everyone else*.

As is, the market place decides if GMO foods are in circulation, and those who want the cheaper - and times even better tasting foods - are willing to take the exaggerated health risks, can decide to.

We have examples to go by with other countries that have already instituted the food Gestapo. In Britain, for example, they now label tomato paste produced from Genetically Modified tomatoes, and the end result was those marked GMO sold better than the non-GMO variety. Why? Because the taste and price made the final decision for them and that would be the case here in America too.

What to do about Cloning

In the last couple of segments, I was discussing the perceived negative outcomes speculated by the anti-GM foods cartel. With this I can't help but wonder how many of those skeptics advocate for the "Trans-humanist" agenda.

Trans-humanists, basically advocate for the "improvement" of the human species through any means necessary; including genetic manipulation to rush the process of evolution.

Parts of their arguments do have merit, I'll admit. One of the arguments in favor says that many genetic conditions can be neutralized before they can be progressed. If the science sticks to this agenda, then it is worth exploring. The rest of it is simply rhetoric condoning Eugenics. Many in the scientific community ignore the ethical implications completely, while others minimize them as just not understanding the science and situation. Maybe so, but you don't dispel people's legitimate concerns by antagonizing them.

I don't personally advocate cloning and in my opinion the arguments for it are weak at the very least, downright inhumane in the more extreme cases. The common arguments in favor I've come across are:

*That because we manipulate, our environment, our food and animals, human genetic manipulation is acceptable.

*It's going to happen anyway.

The former argument doesn't hold traction at all. Environmental manipulation is as natural as breathing. All animals manipulate their environment to some degree. They build shelters and nests, using twigs, leaves, and whatever else they can find. Others build burrows or use man-made refuse as dens.

Animal testing and manipulation of animal and plant genomes are different from human cloning and manipulation as well, for one reason. Animals don't have rights. Animals operate off of instinct, not reason. In order to be eligible you have to be a being of reason. That might sound callous, but we are the top of the food chain. We need to start acting like it.

The argument with animals works less in their favor all around. We have a type of cloning used today on animals for meat and milk, but it only works for certain species though and a large portion of those cloned suffer debilitating health issues and defects. They lived short and painful lives, even the famous

28

Dolly - the first cloned sheep - lived only about half as long as a naturally born animal. The risks of increases in disease and deformity are high enough that human cloning concerns are valid. Being the top of the food chain means ignoring rationale that is not rational.

Being the top of the food chain is another reason against it as well. Their argument is in favor of increasing intelligence and other traits. Increasing these traits minimizes the playing field and immediately renders their arguments mute. *"All men are created equal."* Does that ring a bell?

This is an argument for creating an *Artificial Equality*; this never works and ends up having long lists of unintended consequences. People are given the exact same opportunities and if they choose to squander those opportunities so be it. It's not ethical (or appears even constitutional) to mess with that.

One of the most insidious ideas of all this is "Therapeutic Cloning," basically this is the making of clones to use as spare parts. This is a prime example of why this research should not be continued, at least not until the ethical implications are addressed.

As for the later argument in favor, this is simply a form of "soft bullying." If it's going to happen, why bother trying to change it? If you could predict when you were going to die, would you try to change that? It's worth trying to change it if it shows signs of being an inhumane and brutal practice without even a clear argument of the societal benefits. The means does not justify the ends and just because you can do something doesn't mean you should.

Sequestration Blues

There was a major bru-ha-ha recently about the proposed sequestration cuts. Those who want to spend your money made the claim that *any* cuts in any department would be an econ-apocalypse.

It hasn't been, in fact the repercussions on the general public have been minor, at worst. For the most part "we the people" have not have any ill effects from these cuts. Among the loudest voices of opposition to the cuts was the government monolith known as the Federal Aviation Administration. They laid claim that cutting their budget was practically impossible and would only lead to major problems, for their passengers. They would be forced to cut their staff and services, the lines would be massive and all would suffer excruciating delays. To this I say - so what?

Man up and take the heat, stop your sniveling like a baby. Correct me if I'm wrong, but isn't that what a competent president of operations of any large company supposed to do? Make the hard decisions of whether or not to cut services and staff, if necessary, to keep the company afloat? In the private sector that's just a reality of doing business, it's sad, but sometimes the only viable course of action.

The public sector, however, doesn't have to obey the rules of practical economics, or what we call "the Real World" (not to be confused with that moronic show on MTV). That's the difference between having to earn your money and having the bill passed to the taxpayer.

More to the point if the president of a company refuses to do those hard choices, the board of directors should fire him, and look for someone who will. That's the first job that should be lost. There are those in the private sector, who will do this, we call them "Capitalists" - find one of them and make them the president of these companies.

We need people who will come up with solutions (at times very unpleasant ones) that will cultivate results to make the companies stronger in the long run. The TSA, GSA, FAA, DOD, and every government agency need to take financial hit and alter their spending habits to a level realistic with the current economic turmoil. The American people already have. The statement being sent here with federal inaction, is the same as in the book *Animal Farm* - "All are created equal, but some are more equal than others."

Killing Elmo

During the 2012 presidential campaign, Mitt Romney took a lot of flak for a comment he made about defunding PBS. It became an easy quip for Obama, making statements that he was trying to kill big bird and similar rhetoric. But the question is was Romney wrong?

Only a few in the media asked that question. Those who didn't ask already knew the answer, they just didn't like the answer. They didn't like it because the public would have supported the idea and to them cutting funding to any federal program equates the death of that program.

But if the program was so essential, why can't they be funded privately? Because only the extremists of the left wing would want to keep it going - and God forbid they put their own money where their big fat mouth is!

The rest of us just aren't smart enough to appreciate the arts, you see, so your tax dollars have to be put where they will do the most good for society. Oh God bless those benevolent and enlightened progressives. I might cry with joy, or maybe that's disgust and revolusion. Judging by that sour taste in the back of my throat, the latter sounds more likely!

This is not the only piece of "art" that you are being forced to endorse without your consent, *The Endowment for the Arts* is full of them. Ever hear of *The Piss Christ?*

Now keep in mind I really don't care how sick and demented a piece of art is - as long as it doesn't cause physical harm of others or involve child porn - it's the artist's right to make whatever statement they want. What I am saying is that I don't want to pay for it. Those who do find these statements objectionable shouldn't have to pay for them either. The other artists should find this objectionable to - they work hard and get ignored, while these shock jocks making statements that are literally pieces of crap get fully funded! Who wouldn't be mad?

MR. Nice Guy

Presidential candidate Mitt Romney received flak by his own party for his statements which included referring to the president as a "nice guy."

He should have been called out on this, but is it really fair for commentators like, Bill O'Reilly or Sean Hannity, to comment about this - since they are guilty of this as well. As much as they may hate Obama's policies his staunchest critics have started their analysis with the phrase, "he might be a nice guy, but…" and then go into their scathing retorts. But I don't do that, because Obama is not only not a good president, but not a "nice guy," he is an arrogant, smarmy elitist, with a God complex. I understand what Romney and others were doing, I think it's wrong is all.

So, what's with the "nice guy" talk? It's because the media loves the guy and for a lot of people if you start off the bat attacking the president his supporters glaze over and shut down. I don't care; my opinion is the president is dangerous and trying to keep his detractors silent. His battle plan is oppression and manipulation and he aims to destroy and conquer - "nice guy" indeed.

Slaves to your Phones

Here's one more choice that people are not always happy with - being afraid of being a slave to technology. That's ridiculous, are we a slave to technology, of course we are. We are completely beholden to our technological advances. But it's not only normal, it's necessary. This is how it's always been, though, we are a creature without fangs, claws or able to produce venom. What took other species millions of years to develop and perfect through evolution, our species has to develop through our continued technological prowess. That is our survival technique, utilizing the materials of the area in the most efficient way.

But think of how amazing our technology has been, in the early days of the computer, it was massive and filled the whole room and did little more than a calculator. Now those features (and many more) are on our cellular phones and the next wave for cell technology is smart phones for your wrist. That's mind blowing when you think how relatively new cell phones are, not being mainstream until the 1990's.

How about TVs, look at the change there. It wasn't even too long ago that TVs were cumbersome and heavy, and flat TVs were rare and expensive - now you can get one for a couple of hundred dollars or less.

The lesson in all this is the same, choices, choices, choices. This is the key to coming up with the best in life, and the way to get choices is the free market not the government.

Chapter TWO

PROHIBITIONS:
LIMITS FOR OUR OWN GOOD?

Just like the alcohol prohibition during the 1930's, modern day prohibitions cause more problems that it fixes. That's because it's morality from one person being imprinted on others, which has no moral weight behind it which causes a black market and rebellion in the people.

Society **structures end up** conforming to **two** different models of justice (with slight variations). Both models can be classified under one simple theory, though, that I call 'Magnet Theory.'

Model one, is the North/South variant. Two different forces of society, the law and the criminal elements, meet. They have different agendas and different needs. One needs order, the other chaos. So through this exchange there is opposition, which in turn creates a type of equilibrium. So law and order is maintained through this balance.

Model two, is the North/North or South/South variant. The same two forces meet again. This time however, they have similar agendas and needs. Both seek power and control, rather than law and order. So through this exchange of similarity, opposition occurs. The result is anarchy and everyone fights with each other.

Examples of the 'Magnet Theory' have been seen throughout world history. In our country, prohibition is an example of a version of Model One.

A law that many disagreed with was introduced into law in the U.S. The result was that those who enforced the law were considered to be in the wrong. The criminals brought back the illegal liquor to the masses and were considered the heroes of the common man. The law abiding citizens helped out and sheltered the criminal element, and in turn the criminals only really hurt those who committed "crimes" against their enterprise or family. So it was the criminals who maintained a sort of law and order. Even during a time of acceptable anarchy, a form of justice can be maintained.

A demonstration of Model Two can be seen with the current states of countries like Mexico, parts of South America and Africa, and parts of the Middle East. The criminal elements (drug cartels, mostly) are either in league with the nation's armies and police forces, or are battling them for supremacy using the citizens as leverage. The police and military in those areas are notorious for operating using oppressive tactics and intimidation. Both sides seek to oppress the citizens instead of enlisting their assistance.

So how does this happen? Why does the Criminal Justice System diverge like this, into either; cooperation between the citizens and either the authorities and criminals, or into the chaotic state of oppression? Well, it has the do with the existence of or absence, of two other elements.

First, (and most important because the second can't occur without this) clear and concise defined laws and ordinances. Without distinct ordinances from the legislators, its citizens, criminals, and law enforcement, don't know what is expected in society. Laws in the, before mentioned, more oppressive countries are vague at best and even if you do obey the statutes you run the risk of detainment because of the rampant corruption in its legal system. The criminal leaders have bought the system and its soldiers have beaten its law enforcers into submission.

Second element needed, is a strong opposition

to whichever force is more domineering of its citizens, to be decided by the citizens. Right or wrong, the criminals were the side the citizens sided with during prohibition because the laws were considered ethically wrong and too intrusive.

So, what's my point here - the prohibition of the 1930's created this bizarre magnetic social structure, through bad laws that only caused more problems. Maybe we should reconsider our original views on prohibitions.

Never Met a Regulation He didn't like

President Obama had made it a major part of his campaign that he would protect small business and the new mandates would only affect them minimally - he lied.

While the scale might not be as large as the national powerhouses of the corporate world, the small business still has to comply with the sweeping current of regulations that have come from this administration. ObamaCare might not have (or when fully implemented, will not) cause many, if any problems for the small business, but that's not all the president has done that will be damaging to business.

Do you know how many new regulations he has added? He's doubled the regulations and restrictions that were already at a demanding level. If you've seen your favorite spots close their door, that's why. Yet the talking points from the White House are that the economy is improving. Really? We haven't recovered the jobs that were lost, few new jobs have been created and we're still at an unacceptable level of unemployment, in the double digits.

But that's the federal government, what about the local levels, they have to be a lot better, right? Yes, but there is still room for improvement, I learned this first hand recently. It was not fun!

I had to go to a licensing board to get a different state occupational license, I wound up having to go to that state (why there was a complication, I'm still not sure) and what should have taken a month took four. What was clear was the board did enjoy their power, as much as a federal bureaucracy.

Things went in my favor in this, but mostly because I played the game. I dressed up, suit and tie, and didn't speak until addressed. But all this has made me wonder, why do we need state licensing? Why isn't a federal one enough? Having another license doesn't make the patrons any safer, there's no advantage for the businessman and it makes moving to a new state more challenging than it should be.

But the stranglehold of red-tape doesn't stop there, it only begins. To operate you need a business license from the state, another expense without any benefit. If you're actually lucky enough to still make a profit after all this and want to expand, then you need a permit with the zoning board - that's right another board to deal with. Depending on the result of that meeting you might have another fee to expand.

This whole process doesn't give any benefit to the entrepreneur and is more about milking them at every available chance and we wonder why all our jobs go overseas. Could there be a connection? Nah!

Did Joe Camel really do it?

How often do you hear cancer activists stand up for the smoker? How about conservative activists who claim they want less government interference in our lives?

This is an issue that both the left and right seem to be in agreement - the smokers have got to go! Even Obama, a former smoker himself, has no sympathy for them. That's harsh, man. This is one of those issues that sketchy science is used to push legislature that is based more on virtue than the law.

It's the virtue that changes depending on the side you're on, with the right it's about the effect on the body as a temple. It's a sin to smoke, so it's right to prohibit people using the law, right. Nope! The law is set up to protect our legal rights not guide others behavior. As long as we don't harm others, then so be it. Wait - what about secondhand smoke and all those who are dying of cancer from it? That's harming a lot of innocent people isn't it? That's where the science gets sketchy, the "Secondhand Smoke" theory has been reviewed and found to be rarer than claimed. For the most part it has more to do with lawyers trying to line their own pockets, than any real danger to the public.

Now on the left side, this is a lot more complicated - the claim has to do with keeping costs down in healthcare, but the real reason has nothing to do with ObamaCare - it's a profitable industry that doesn't ask for government assistance and that can't be allowed. The modern argument is that smokers use up a lot of health services resources, but that's not true. They use less.

The way it really works is like this; smokers go in for a check-up, they get diagnosed with cancer most will be told there's nothing that can be done; if they past this stage they are moved into another demographic, that the doctors still can't do anything for; and this cycle continues, using inexpensive tests until you get down to those who can be helped with treatment or transplants, a meager 8%. All those who can't be treated don't add to the burden on healthcare though, they lessen it, since they die early and won't use up resources. The problem is that means there is one less person in the "risk pool", which the Affordable Care Act (ObamaCare) is dependent on. That's why, to the Democrats, the smoker is so dangerous.

Whether it's over virtue or profit, the tobacco industry is an easy target, but in the end no matter, what it's the smoker that pays the highest price.

Open Mind, Open Debate, Open Border

There are certain issues that people are unwilling to even discuss. Why? Why is the mere mention of the possibilities, really that horrendous? Is the fact that they might be wrong really so inconceivable?

Well, that might be the case here. In the list of unmentionable truths are: abortion, gun control, gay marriage and immigration reform. Gun control, is easy, it's unconstitutional to do it. The right to keep and bear is arms are not to be infringed. End of debate, so let's move on.

The rest of the issues are not much trickier. These are states' rights issues. That's were the biggest part of the debate should conclude, but it doesn't. Many think the government has the burden of responsibility to decide these issues; they don't even have the *right* to decide them really. It's the right of the states, to decide and a national uniform standard rule of law doesn't benefit the states or the country as a whole. This includes immigration. When a federal position has been implemented it over-rides the states' rights of enforcing their laws, that's the flaw in federalism. If anything the federal policy we should be fighting for is open borders. The founding fathers saw the importance of not obstructing on immigrants coming in, and that's where we have gotten it wrong.

In creating these restrictions on legal immigration we have manufactured a massive, convoluted mess, which rewards those who cross illegally and punishes those playing by the rules. The wait to become a citizen on average is 10 years and I understand the application is quite extensive. Much of this includes a thorough knowledge of American history. Now not to down-play the importance of learning history, but why should those coming into the country be required to learn it when most natives' knowledge of the subject is - shall we say - anemic?

Many are all too eager to demonize those that claim we need to reform our immigration policy and just need to enforce the laws we have, but we do need reform. The problem is that no one is addressing the flaws in the policy. Most just want to put up a massive wall surrounding the country. Keep in mind that's also what pretty much every socialist and communist leader thought was a good idea too - the pigs in their pen. The pigs being of course his oppressed people. Doesn't that kind of concern people? An alternative to this is bringing the troops home and placing them along the border, doesn't that sound better?

I'm not saying to let everyone in or even let all who come in to become full citizens, but if you look at the idea of a work program free from emotional absolutism, it kind of makes sense. Right now there are jobs that are being filled by immigrants that Americans won't (and thanks to the unions can't take) for the pay being offered. It's sad but true. Many American citizens would rather be pan-handlers than get a real job.

This conclusion that I came to did not come easily, but all the evidence points that way. If we want to have a positive immigration policy, we should first end the war on drugs and the entitlements system (for American born citizens and immigrants both). I disagree with anyone getting benefits if they don't contribute to the system when they can.

While I'm for immigration reform, I'm

against the recent bill on immigration. What I'm concerned about it is what they have tacked on in the bill, it's over two thousand pages remember. What else is in it? Any bill that is more than a hundred pages should be voted down, for that reason.

To sum things up - if an issue has valid concerns and no real solutions, than it should be up for an open debate. As things sit, it appears that both the border and the debate will remain closed.

The Wall that will Never be Built

As well as being somewhat questionable an idea, there's another larger concern with the border security fence. Who's going to build it?

The Republican Party? - It hasn't happened under them yet. They have been the only ones showing interest in it, or so they claim. After the comments by analysts, who really thinks it's going to be built now? I don't, they won't run the risk of alienating the Hispanic vote.

So, how about the Democrats? They never wanted the fence to begin with. At least on this issue they have been honest.

So that leaves the independent parties, but most of them don't want it either. The reason for them is that it's really expensive and more than likely won't work. Frankly it's not a very good plan and pursuing it is throwing good money after bad. Besides

43

the government is more concerned with hindering American citizens, putting roadblocks inside the country, rather than a wall around it. Internal policy reforms are a better strategy.

Minimum Wage and the Immigration Connection

At the time of this writing, our nation is in the midst of a strike of the fast food industry. To those protesters this is a word of caution against it.

There are many problems they have not considered. First, the companies are going to cut somewhere in their budgets, which means kiss your benefits good-bye.

Second, the workforce itself will have to be massively cut to survive; many will have to close its doors for good. Keep in mind it's not only the large chains that have to comply with these laws - but the little mom & pop shops, and franchises as well - who simply can't afford it.

Third, these jobs were never supposed to be careers - but stepping stones to something better - and if they have to pay $17 an hour they are going to recruit the brightest and the best. If you don't have a bachelor's degree, don't bother applying at *McDonald's!*

Don't you feel a little guilty for taking these jobs from the kids who need them for work experience? Don't you strive for a higher quality job? Not many would consider fast food to be of high aspirations. That's why it's for first timers and immigrants. But if these protesters get their way it will only one demographic that will get these jobs - illegal immigrants. The teenagers, legal immigrants, and even the protesters will lose their jobs en masse, because $17 an hour isn't feasible. It won't work, that's the bottom line!

If the employers have to abide by this they will maximize their workforce by hiring the group who are exempt from this restrictive law. Good job cutting your own throats!

Legal Monopoly

When people get in trouble they get them a board certified attorney, without even considering the other options. They could try to learn the law of their case themselves and represent themselves. They could consider bringing in a paralegal.

This is a mindset that attorneys advance at every opportunity, you need a real attorney, and the other options won't help you. But it doesn't end there, as well as keeping all other options away with this propaganda; they start the prohibition process in their very education.

To be fair to the purveyors of the legal system they do go through a lot to get there, which may have

45

to do with the monopolistic grasp of the market. They crowd others out because they didn't make the sacrifice of years of their lives and a small fortune exceeding $100,000. Modern lawyers learned to edge out the competition in law school, it was not in the classroom - but by the example of the *American Bar Association*, their influence in other law schools, with their strict regulations and accreditation process has not gone unnoticed.

The ABA faculty makes the decisions for all other laws schools from budget, admissions, courses offered, to the faculty. Both the faculty and courses offered at law schools, have risen exponentially - even though the occupation is suffering a decline, part of that is due to the regulations mentioned but also because the new courses offered are unrealistic to the real world client base, unless they are a hard-core social activist. Online learning is basically absent as well, and the curriculum amounts to a total of 58,000 minutes required for graduating, 45,000 of it in a physical classroom.

So, what's the cost of all this regulation? Applications are down almost 50% across the country. The *National Association for Law Placement* reports only about 65% of graduates from 2011 have landed law-related employment within nine months of graduating, further demoralizing entering into the profession. The highest cost of all this, the lack of flexibility in the real world scenarios, no mechanism for testing new methods of conducting the law for the needs of the future - and it is one more mark in the ledger of a long and expanding list of educational institutions and businesses run in a very mafia-esque manner. It goes to show that in the realm of higher learning that the less is more approach is still outside the elite's intellectual grasp.

Marijuana by any Other Form will Still Get you High... Not True

In the polls the number is about 58% of the general public want to end the restrictions on this drug. This has led to a backlash by politicians adamantly opposed to the lifting of these bans, in some cases to violate their own states laws. Creating agencies within their states to keep their citizenry from making the "wrong" choices when it comes to their own medical care. Case in point, Chris Christie of New Jersey, would rather let a two year suffer and die painfully, than let her have the legally prescribed medications.

Because of the long held mentality of the drug war, many are led to believe that the only medical benefit this plant is in pain relief, but research into it has proven that this is false. How do we get from a hallucinatory, perception altering drug, into a beneficial treatment for some fairly serious ailments? Modern medical science utilizing chemistry is how. Chemists simply broke down the chemical makeup, altered it and developed a completely new plant with new possibilities.

47

To understand how this works you have to know what causes the effects from marijuana. The chemical is called THC and changing the chemical is the key; alter this by removing the T you modify the effects from it, remove the H you alter it another way, and so on.

The case with Christie is that a New Jersey resident's two year old daughter has been prescribed a High C variant to treat her epilepsy, this variant it should be noted does not have the hallucinatory effects and reduces the seizures. Christie would rather let this child die - in a state where marijuana is legal - than follow up on the science in this issue.

There have been many scientific studies on the benefits of this plant, 34 that back up its usefulness in lessening the symptoms as well as being a pain reliever. Still not convinced, well consider this - let's take another known drug; unprocessed we have poppy seeds, processed we have morphine, opium or heroin. Morphine is a legal pain reliever that is more dangerous and more addictive, than marijuana. Penicillin is another medication that is dangerous if not altered from its original form. In fact our entire medical industry depends on our making potentially dangerous substances into a beneficial one.

The point is this is not a case of drug addicts trying to score for their fix that's being blocked by the law because of the question whether incarceration or treatment is more effective, this is a case of people who have been prescribed a medical treatment, with a pompous ideology infringing on the doctor patient privilege.

There may be Side Effects

As is the case with drug usage - legal or not - the act of prohibiting drugs has had serious side effects. In the case of all prohibitions there has been the formation of black markets, on rare occasions the black markets make society function better, but the vast majority increase violence and have other negative consequences for society - such as the effects from the Magnet Theory, mentioned earlier.

Another side effect not talked about nearly enough is the appearance of alternatives, which include black market clinics for abortions; and in countries with socialized medicine illegal healthcare clinics; in gun control, 3D printing and alternatives for the rounds, using wax or hot glue - but the alternatives for drugs are downright scary.

Bath salts and Meth have been around awhile now, but now another synthetic drug has made it to the United States - *Krokodil*.

The drug Krokodil, has been used in Russia for years, but has only recently appeared in Arizona and a few other states; and like bath salts and meth, uses common everyday household items to make it - and has extreme side effects. One of the side effects of Krokodil is the one that gives it its name; a physical skin deformity that resembles crocodile scales.

These synthetic drugs are the best reason to reconsider our drug laws, not only are the alternatives more dangerous for the user's body, but are more dangerous for the communities.

The ingredients in making the synthetics are highly flammable and could eventually make a whole town unlivable, because of the gasses emitted during their processing. In the war on drugs it appears we forgot to read the list of side effects.

We have a Problem with Perception

The general public is so easy to manipulate by the press - mostly because they know their Achilles heel. When a national tragedy unfolds that they don't want to cover - for fear of embarrassing the president - they simply find a more benign social issue that is tied to abandoned virtue.

Take the Miley Cyrus controversy, in her performance she let her co-performer dryhump her and everyone goes nuts! Maybe I'm really jaded, but in the larger picture making such a big deal about this is … well, stupid.

It's the MTV music awards first off; this is just par for the course of that venue. MTV has been on the decline anyways, since it has become a haven for the most trite "reality" shows on TV. This debacle was a boon for them so their plan worked, and the fact that it was so effective kind of proves my point. With everything else that is going on why is the nation so fixated on this? Rather than having a discussion on Syria, curtailing federal spending, the ethics of the entitlement culture, or the disaster ObamaCare; what possible significance does a hyper-sexualized diva have in this melodrama? Unfortunately it serves as a distraction.

If this should have been covered at all it should have been as a news blip. One of the puff pieces by the pop culture magazines in grocery store checkout lines, *not a story to be covered all week by the national media.*

Understand I'm not condoning what she did, frankly, I don't really care. What I'm saying is there are far bigger problems that garner our national attention than this and to be completely candid, focusing on it will only ensure that it will happen again. Shock beats reality, style beats substance. That's the way the game is played and it looks to be that the nation just got "sorry-ed."

Do Speed Limits really Work?

One of the ways to escape from conventional wisdom is to ask questions about all our institutions. This is a perfect example - Do speed limits really work?

Well, here's what I found out.

First, I checked out the death rates on the *Autobahn,* the stretch of road in Germany that has no speed limit. The annual death toll is about 800 people a year.

51

Then I checked that against the number of deaths in the United States each year, which are around 12,000. That's a big difference, but is it significant? Not yet, no. This is a very unbalanced comparison, like weighing a watermelon against a grape and calling that a valid weight test. So let's go to a smaller scale - check the data on single roads.

There are roads in the US that have equal or even higher death rates than the Autobahn. One road in Alaska has an annual death toll of about 1,000 drivers. It's not designed as efficiency as the Autobahn however, and most of the deaths are more likely due to that. The *Autobahn* is a smooth ride with few turns through the countryside. Some of the deaths could be contributed to distracted driving, because of its serenity.

To finish off this study you have to know what is different about the Autobahn; to go on it you have to get a specific drivers training, a special driver's permit which is expensive and the cars in Germany are designed for those kinds of speeds.

So do speed limits works? Possibly, but I still think that an *Autobahn* could work here in the states. In the meantime watch out for speed traps.

No Pets Allowed

Many apartment complexes have listings that include "no smoking or pets allowed." For the most part the restrictions are for the same reason, possible destruction of property - this still doesn't make it right.

To be fair if you talk to your landlord you might get an exception, depending on the animal. If it's like say a fish in a small tank or bowl or some kind of reptile, its doubtful many landlords would object and in the worst cases you might have to pay more in rent. If you can prove you need the animal for mental stability, they legally have to let you keep the animal.

These restrictions are questionable, but perfectly acceptable, it's the free market in action - it's when the state objects to it that there's a problem. As much as I lobby for the tenth amendment, even state legislature can be wrong and the laws on pets are debatable.

For a long time you couldn't keep ferrets in California, now you can keep them but not breed them there. Many states have laws that prohibit individuals not involved with educational occupations from keeping "potentially dangerous" animals, such as poisonous reptiles or large carnivores.

The claims of these restrictions are that if the animal is released or escapes it could deplete food resources or the native wildlife. It's a reasonable assumption, make a law to keep dangerous animals away from irresponsible people - there's nothing wrong with that, or is there? It also punishes those who do know how to handle these animals safely and that's not right for responsible pet owners.

As for the laws efficiency, that too is up for debate. There are still many unwanted pets that are simply abandoned rather than taken to local pet shops, animal shelters or the local Department of Wildlife - Why? Because if people are caught in possession of these animals they are penalized. Try this instead, rather than a system encouraging them to hide the animals - that they will release if they don't want it or don't want to get caught with it - encourage the owners to turn the animal in, without a lecture or legal reprisal, if they no longer want the animal or can't keep it. That will cut back on, if not eliminate the practice of releasing unwanted pets and we won't have to be concerned about our native wildlife being hurt by an invading species. Turning back pet prohibition is something that the animal kingdom would approve of.

Let it Roll

In the eyes of many, gambling is immoral, but should there be a law against it? The federal government thought so, and passed the *Illegal Gambling Act of 1970*, which basically says that "any betting of $2,000 or more in a single day, against five or more people, if it's against state or local laws is considered an illegal gambling operation and punishable by up to ten years in prison.

　　Why do we need this law? Why is the state government even interfering in this, let alone the federal government? Because it's a sin - but don't we have the right to make our own choices of personal morality? It doesn't hurt anyone, does it?

No, but its enforcement has - Sal Culosi knows how serious this law can be. In 2005, Culosi was in a Virginia bar, betting with a drinking buddy on a local college football game. A local cop heard him and in an effort to get him on an easy arrest, got Culosi to up the ante to that $2,000 mark. Eventually he did and Culosi was greeted by a SWAT team at his doorstep to bring him in, in the encounter Culosi was shot through the heart. The question, that comes up - were the actions of the cop unethical? He basically encouraged Culosi to break the law; doesn't that make him partially culpable of Culosi's actions? Yes, Culosi is a responsible adult, but the officer knows the law and was taking advantage of Culosi.

If a businessman had done something like this, the watchdogs would have screamed foul and rightly so. When it comes to morality laws it looks like the people of the United States have drawn a losing hand.

Could I get a Kidney Please?

On the list of taboo topics it appears there is one I forgot to mention. For some reason that has never really made much sense people find it distasteful, immoral or downright ... disturbing, to even broach the idea of selling your organs.

The laws match this sentiment and in order to donate you have to convince the hospital staff that you're doing it as an act of altruism rather than for compensation. One question - why is it any of their business? So what, if someone is so hard up for cash they want to sell a part of their body? How is that anybody else's concern?

According to the opponents of organ selling it's because the donors are being exploited. Exploited? In what way? They're getting paid for a good, how are they being exploited? Now if someone was holding a friend or relative hostage with the demands - you donate your kidney or say good-bye to your loved one that would be exploitation. See the difference?

This is probably the clearest example of *Virtue Absolutism* there is. If you go in to any hospital, in almost any country, (except Iran, oddly enough) and so saying you're donating an organ to be a good person, good ahead. Go in there and tell them you want to sell an organ, because you're eating dog food to get by, they will slap the cuffs on you.

Another point to consider - how is this any different from selling your blood? Or sperm or eggs? It's still tissue, it's still a part of you - so, how is it any less immoral? But for some reason it is.

The thing is I think out of any we should receive payment for, it's organs. With blood or bone marrow the donor has a very low risk of complications; with an organ the risk is substantially higher. It's a major surgery and chances are good you'll die on the table - even with the improved modern technology. With those levels of increased risk, shouldn't we give every incentive for people to do the right thing, at their our discretion? For making such a potentially fatally choice, isn't it reasonable to expect to be paid? I think so.

It's an odd thing to me that so many capitalists are opposed to this, because this is a very capitalist idea.

The Red Tape before Getting Ink

Considering getting that new tattoo that you saved all summer to get? Maybe you're turning eighteen and want to celebrate your coming of age with a navel piercing. Or you want to mark a memorable moment like beating cancer or the birth of your first child. Well, you may have to endure for a little longer, a twenty-four hour waiting period, to be more precise. At least that will be the case if the Department of Health's new guidelines get turned into law.

Straight from the government to you:

204 PRE-OPERATING PROCEDURES - WAITING PERIOD, TATTOOS &BODY-PIERCINGS *
204.1 The licensee or operator of a body art establishment shall ensure that no tattoo artist applies any tattoo to a customer until after twenty-four (24) hours have passed since the customer first requested the tattoo.

204.2 The licensee or operator of a body art establishment shall ensure that no body- piercer shall body-pierce a customer until after twenty-four (24) hours have passed since the customer first requested the body-piercing.

204.3 The licensee or operator shall ensure that no body artist or body art establishment shall bind or attempt to bind a customer to committing to obtaining a tattoo or body- piercing, or bind or attempt to bind a customer into paying for a tattoo or body- piercing upon signing the Twenty-four (24) Hour Waiting Period Acknowledgment Form.

Why are they butting in on this issue, well, because they know best remember? In fact, that is the reason given to the *Washington Post*, by Najma Roberts of the Department of Health:

> *"We're making sure when the decision is made that you're in the right frame of mind, and you don't wake up the next morning... Oh my god, what happened?"*

Oh isn't that great how they are looking for you? Actually I find it downright creepy. Just when you think the government can't find another part of our lives to concern itself with... Surprise!

I'm sure some readers of this segment are wondering - hey what's the big deal? So you have to wait for a day to get a tattoo or piercing? That's not the point; the problem is that the government is dictating a very personal choice that is frankly none of their business. Look at the reason given what does that have to do with the *Department of Health*? How is this a health risk? Tattoos and piercing are perfectly safe if done right.

This is about control. If they start down this road where will it end? Will they start saying what tattoos are illegal? Saying how many you can legally have? Or worse will they start to order you to get a tattoo, like oppressive governments in the past have to mark the "inferior" of the society. I'm not saying that any of those things *will* happen, but how can you be so sure it *won't*?

This is one more decision that is being taken away from you and those in charge have already done away with so many. What you can put into your body; the stupid things you should be allowed to do; your privacy; the prices of goods and services, because of regulations; your choices with your children; your choices in morality and now your right at self-expression. Where will this madness end? Will those who make the choices for us ever be satisfied? Or is this a continuous loop of oppression?

Lastly where does Obama stand on this? He made his opinion clear when he said that if his daughters ever got a tattoo he and Michelle would go out and get the exact same ones. What happened to the "rock star" president who was so new age and progressive? He and McCain are sounding more and more alike all the time. So why did we even bother with the farce of an election if we get the same thing either way.

Chapter **THREE**

WAR ON WARS

War is not given the respect it is due. If it were it would be declared with more restraint. The biggest problem with war, it is when the people will voluntarily give up their rights.

That is why the "State of Emergency", is so popular with legislature; they can pass their agendas with little resistance from the constituency.

War is not only used in cases of foreign policy it is declared for social issues as well. It is not enough that we have to instigate destructive international policy because of this little word, but now when a politician has a whim he invokes emotional manipulation to make sure their bill gets passed.

War on Wars

I **would consider myself** anti-war, by the definition of the term as I understand it at any rate. War should be used in restraint, approved through congress and only used as a last resort, not the first course of action. But it's not enough that war - the violent, physical struggle between two nations - should be used in restraint, but the very word war should be used with more restraint.

Because of the emotional connection of the word "war" it has been as cavalierly used as the literal meaning. We have the *War on Poverty,* the *War on Drugs,* the *War on Terror,* the *War on Women,* the *Culture War*, how about we add a new one to the mix - *The War on War*, both the literal and verbal forms. Both forms should be used with more discussion and forethought, instead of being used with such recklessness. No more going to war under lazy arguments or when we don't have a direct stake in it.

Wars are costly and are used to control people, and there should be more consideration to other options.

The word war is used to soft bully the citizens into acceptance of policies that go against their best interests or tell them it's their responsibility to give up their rights. Their real responsibility is to make sure they keep their rights and pass them on to the next generation. There are direct correlations between the verbal and literal wars, in the way of their intention of those abusing them anyway. They are used less to protect people and more to enslave them.

Why so Tense?

In the list of speakers on the anniversary of Martin Luther King's epic march on Washington was King's daughter, Bernice King.

Her speech was on the same level as her predecessor relative and was the only one worth listening to - all the rest, the president included were all spouting the race-baiting verbal diarrhea that has spread across the country. Going on the same old tape loop; Trayvon Martin was murdered, racial inequality is rampant, and voter ID laws are racially motivated - blah, blah, blah! Actually I guess it's closer to - Baahh, baahh, baahh! Does the grass taste better on that side of the fence? - It's probably all the fertilizer. Opps, there's a weed, I think it's called an "Independent Thought" better hurry and kill it, it spreads fast.

Trayvon and the racial inequality myths I'll get to later in this chapter, but for this segment I want to go into the voter ID myth. Show me in the constitution were it says that we have the right to vote. Go on do right now, I'll wait.

Okay, ready? How about Amendment XIV, Section II,

"*Representatives shall be appointed among the several States according to their respective numbers... But when the right to vote at any election for the choice of the electors for President and Vice President of the United States.*"

I know you're thinking it says right there, "*right to vote*," so I'm wrong, right? Read it again. That's for the *elector*, the person who votes for the president and vice president for you; you don't vote for the President or Vice President themselves.

Next!... Amendment XV, Section I,

"*The right of citizens of the United States to vote shall not be denied or abridged by the United States or any State on account of race, color, or previous condition of servitude.*"

That gives the minorities at least the right to vote doesn't it? Not exactly, they can't be *discriminated* from voting because of ethnicity (and at that time for being a freed slave) but it doesn't stipulate the right to vote itself.

One last try, do you feel lucky? Amendment XIX,

"*The rights of citizens of the United States to vote shall not be denied or abridged by the United States or by any State on account of sex.*"

This is the same as Amendment XV, Section I, they can't be discriminated because of gender, not the right to vote itself. It makes sense that progressive race-baiters and feminists push this narrative; it falls into their philosophy of manufactured equality quite nicely. Manufactured equality is not true equality though and gives one group an advantage, something that its supporters claim to be fighting against. So if you think you have the right to vote, then you - like Jesse Jackson, Al Sharpton and the others in the race and feminist trenches - are, one, two, three, strikes and you're out!

Desperation Causes more Crime than Poverty

Lyndon Johnson instituted the policy of Social Welfare, under the implication that poverty raises the rate of crime. That however doesn't explain why those in the higher economic brackets commit criminal acts.

I contest the connection of poverty and criminal behavior as being false based on the evidence and I state the true reason behind violations of laws is because of Desperation. Desperation can come in different forms and outcomes from different needs due to our life experiences. Desperate for opportunity, desperate for money, desperate for attention, desperate for love, this proves a far more complete theorem without all the holes in the hypothesis.

But Johnson didn't actually give this any contemplation either way. His reasons for taking this route was purely political, he wanted to be seen as a champion of Civil Rights, as his predecessor John Kennedy was. The problem is all the evidence points to Johnson being a racist. Any conclusion he would have made, would be tainted by this bias, so his policies are that of segregation not of assimilation. Not all those who advocate segregation are racists though. This is a standard based on the common consensus of the era, and it's wrong to make judgments on those from the past based on the standards of our era, that's not what I'm doing. I'm basing them on the standards of his era.

Another example of this Desperation is serial killer Charles Manson. He had a horrible life, devoid of any emotion support, because he wasn't given any to begin with. He was the unwanted son of a prostitute and was basically left to fend for himself. Now I'm not using this to excuse his actions, just explain them. Personally I think he should have been executed, but what's done is done.

Bill and Hillary Clinton are both examples of this as well. What they are in need of is the most dangerous and corrupting of all, the need for power and authority. While Bill might have been the face of the presidency, it was Hillary that really made most of the decisions during that segment of human history. Fortunately, for all of us in order for Bill to get reelected he had to become a Pragmatist and alter his philosophies a little bit.

This one is unfortunately not an uncommon trait for political leaders. Many domestic and foreign have had it. Theodore Roosevelt, Woodrow Wilson, Jimmy Carter, Adolf Hitler, Richard Nixon, Josef

Stalin, Napoleon Bonaparte, Saddam Hussein, Osama Bin Laden, and Barack Obama, just to name a few. We could speculate as to whether any of these men had the intention of becoming the enslavers of their countrymen, but I see that as immaterial personally. They had a need for power and they did what they felt they had to do satisfy that need - simple as that.

This is also the key in addiction as well. An addict has some need in their life not being fulfilled, so they try to numb all emotion with drugs. I contend that with most drugs humans can internally consume without getting addicted... so long as they are not in a vulnerable emotional state. This goes with all addiction as well, not just drugs.

We all know that people do some usual things when we are depressed, would it really be that big of a leap, to consider it the reasons for our shortcomings. We need to accept responsibly for our actions, I'm not trying to excuse anyone with this concept. I'm saying that utilizing this might be useful in helping those that suffer with such problems find solutions.

What Inferiority

Maybe it's because of the careers I've worked in, but I don't see the vast inferiority that is said to be a major crisis in America. There have been both women and minorities that have been both my superiors in the workplace. I've been passed over for deserved promotions by women as well as men.

I've had to deal with discrimination in one of my career fields, because it's not considered common for a guy to be in it. There are jobs out that still have stigmas connected to them depending on gender: for men - it's massage therapists and nurses, for women - it's hard labor positions and tattoo artists, as examples. Does this discrimination suck - yeah, it does, but can it be changed? To a degree, by getting the reliable information out there and changing the minds of the populace.

The question is - what causes these discriminations and are they really discriminations at all? The short answer is in some cases, but not all, most of the time it's practical market principles at work.

Women are generally not in the job market as long, they leave to have children and raise their families. But I have also see in some of the jobs I've worked where there is heavy lifting and fixing equipment, things that the women there called "a man's job."

Those parts of the job are hard on the body and are what put the guys at an "advantage" over their women counterparts. Men and the market aren't taking advantage of women, women voluntarily abdicate an advantage for one reason or another and the men pick up the slack.

This is not discrimination, but market principles giving the one who is willing to do more, make more money. When discriminations do come in a career field they are at the personal discretion of the supervisor or the customer - the supervisor who doesn't promote you because you don't get along or the customer who won't go to a massage therapist because of their gender.

Discrimination is based on personal feelings, not on trying to do what is best for the company or career field. Unfortunately, from time to time discrimination will occur, but it's better that we suffer than we give up another freedom.

Let's Castrate them All

That is the war cry of feminists everywhere, all men are the enemy and should be at the very least sterilized, if not outright slaughtered - or least that's what it was during the 60's.

But like every movement they have mellowed in the rhetoric to a more subtle tactic - if we can't kill men, let's change them. Turn men into women in a way, by making an atmosphere where boys are publicly sanctioned targets - and we all know where the bulls' eye is aimed!

As with every movement there are also people there to capitalize on it, the entrepreneur and feminist, Todd Goldman.

Goldman started his line of anti-boys T-shirts in 1999 with the "Boys are Smelly" product line, which expanded into gems like "Boys are stupid, throw rocks at them!", "Boys tell lies, poke them in the eyes!" or "The stupid factory, where boys are made" and has grown to include other products as well, such as mugs, key chains and posters.

The product line started a controversy in 2003, when a L.A. radio host, Kevin Sacks initiated a campaign against Goldman and his company. This drew activists on both sides; feminists making the charge that if the T-shirts were anti-girl, that the issue would not garner the same level of indignation and that one feminist supported the T-shirts as revenge for boys "bullying", (yeah, that's REAL mature) and another claiming the issue as "unimportant."

This is important in the fact it further divides the sexes, which is the feminist end goal. Somewhere along the way the feminist went from the goal of equal treatment; to that of, death to all men; to, let's make men into women.

The absurdity of the feminist movement had even censored the scientific inquiry into the question of the biological difference of the two genders. Previously when journalists would pitch to investigate this, their bosses deemed it "off limits." Seriously? - A basic and fundamental question of who we are is considered, TABOO?

The question has finally been asked and the differences are more than superficial, with major differences in how our brains operate and analyze information - but that's only logical, look at the difference in behavior.

That's why the different ways boys and girls are raised has evolved. You can raise both genders in the same home, with access to the same toys, in general little boys will play war and the little girls will still want to play with Barbie.

That is what the children have chosen for generations. While I do have respect for those who question institutions and traditions - but in this case the feminists are trying to get little kids to go against their nature, and that's plain wrong.

Unspoken War

There are a lot of laws that should not have been passed, because they give the federal government more authority and take it away from the states, among them are DOMA, No Child Left Behind, the Patriot Act, the Affordable Care Act, the Controlled Substances Act, the Brady Bill, the Fairness Doctrine, to name a few.

Those are laws that we have heard about, though, the one that is going to talked about is this segment hasn't gotten much media attention - but it should because it affects the most important of rights, the freedom of speech. It's called the *Media Shield Law* and as is common with many of the before mentioned laws, it was sold as a law that helps those that it really penalizes.

Its advertised intention is to protect journalists and bloggers, but it hurts both, bloggers the most. It increases regulations on journalists and requires bloggers to have to obtain a business license.

So what? How is that an obstruction? Because

bloggers are not journalists, they are everyday blue-collar workers who are simply trying to get their views out there. This law, along with the internet tax, only serves to censor bloggers - the information ages equivalent to the pamphleteers.

Bloggers are the new independent media - which is why we are deemed a threat. We don't give in to special interests or lobbyists; we offer a smorgasbord of new innovative ideas. To the status quo republicans and democrats we are the biggest threat to their agenda. That's why they want the Media Shield so bad - in the battle of opposing ideas the internet is the Alamo. We may be surrounded but we are not defeated yet.

15 Minutes or less, could save you from your Freedom of Speech

The current administration has more influence in the insurance industry than merely the extreme intrusions of the Affordable Care Act; it has also captured the sympathies of the heads of that particular market as well.

The first showing of this was a couple of years ago, when R. Lee Ermey was at his annual Toys for Tots charity event and actually thought he had the right to speak his mind -

"... I got to tell you folks we have a big problem this

year, the economy really sucks. Now I hate to point fingers at anybody, but the present administration has something to do with that... and I think we should raise up and we should stop this administration from what it's doing, because they are destroying this country. They are driving us into bankruptcy so they can impose socialism on us...."

His punishment for this was that his contract with GEICO insurance was canceled. While I don't personally consider President Obama a socialist (that's not to say that he hasn't involved himself in industries in a despotic manner, he is a dictator of sorts, but socialists at least have a basic under-standing of practical economics that the president doesn't possess) but if that's the word Ermey thinks best suits the man, so be it - celebrities, privately and publicly, have been critical of previous administrations without suffering retribution, at times even being rewarded for it.

I don't think either action is appropriate really, they should not be rewarded or punished - it's an *opinion*, it should have consequences! Another example of this kind of aberrant censorship happened recently when Sean Hannity called the Healthcare.gov hotline for a more benign conversation, but it was the truth. The woman would have been fired anyway, for taking his call. Now, it would be easy to be critical of my analysis on this - this is only a couple of examples, for one thing - but these are two examples of *extreme* over reactions.

Who's George Zimmerman?

When a poll was taken of the general public's following of current events - they were asked the same question from two different angles. They were asked their opinion about the George Zimmerman trial and what they thought about the case. Basically they were indifferent to the case. They just didn't care or didn't recognize his name. Then they were asked about Trayvon - they could not be angrier. They felt that he shouldn't have been killed and his killer was a racist and should face justice. But wait a minute... didn't they say they didn't care about George Zimmerman? How can they be indifferent and yet angry about the same case?

Well, mostly it's because they don't really have any original emotion or thought on the matter. They are told by the media what to feel and in the race war, truth and justice are irrelevant. All that really matters is that the cause of social justice keeps on trucking.

That all this hate and division keeps going so the race baiting Sheperds can tend their ignorant flock. This is so all those Jesse Jacksons and Al Sharptons can spread their poisonous doctrine of racism (they call it *Reverse Racism*, but that's a misnomer, because the reversal of intolerance of any kind is acceptance - which *Reverse Racism* is not!) and keep the fortunes they have gained by making sure none of us have a meaningful discussion. If we

72

did have a real discussion about all this, would the feelings about the Trayvon Martin killing be different?

Trayvon was a gang-banger and criminal, he did bad things and was known as a menace in his neighborhood. In short he had no respect for human life and was not someone to be admired. George Zimmerman was a pillar of the community, he tried to improve the area and eliminate racism. Okay, maybe both those examples are stretches, so was labeling Zimmerman guilty before we even knew what had happened.

So should we remember Trayvon and forget Zimmerman, or should it be vice versa?

FROM THE "OBAMA-NATION": A Study of Class Warfare in America

Before delving into the topic I feel that coming up with a concise and clear definition of the vague terminology is pertinent.

CLASS WARFARE: The Calculated and deliberate effort by those in the higher brackets of the socio-economic or political elite, to hinder or completely barricade, those in the lower brackets from rising up from their economic status.

Keep this definition in mind during the study of this topic, being presented here.

During the time of an impartial investigation of the Benghazi attacks, leaving an ambassador dead, Secretary of State - Hillary Clinton was absent. She wasn't even in the country. What was she doing? Was she overseas trying to smooth over a contentious matter? Maybe discussing the importance of alternative energy to foreign interests? How about just a meeting to discuss ANYTHING of a political nature with a dignitary? None of the above - she was in Australia for a wine tasting event.

Now the criticism by pundits was her absence for questioning on the Benghazi matter, but I say there is something even more chilling about her actions here.

It's just one more example of the attitude of over-indulgence, at the cost of the taxpayer's expense. The ever growing laundry list of impropriety that has been allowed to run rampant, the GSA's extravagant Las Vegas trips, the trip to Hawaii for a Summit - by government agencies.

On an episode of Follow the Money, on *Fox News Business*, host Eric Bolling, suggested that those on Obama's staff should take a pay cut to help ease the public's financial burden. This seems like a perfectly reasonable solution to me, considering that they and their boss have a large portion of the culpability in the downturn in the country's economic state.

How about the holiday celebration with the celebrities the Obama's had one year at the White House - it had elaborate performances by Tim Burton and Johnny Depp, with the theme being *Alice in Wonderland*.

Why is it such a bad thing? In and of itself it's not, but it's the exclusivity of it that could be a sign of elitism on their part. On the guest list of this little jamboree was the families of close friends and acquaintances of the first family. I guarantee if it were put together by the Romney clan or even George Bush and family, the families of the service men and women, or maybe children from the orphanages would have been there.

Christmas in the Obama White House wasn't any less a showing of perceived status. The family set a record for hosting the most Christmas trees in the White House - Thirty seven.

Without regard for the suffering of the common man the Obamas dine on such extravagances as lobster, paid for by the taxpayer.

In conclusion, some who will read this may dismiss this as just hyperbole by someone with an axe to grind about Barack Obama, that's not the case at all. I do believe Obama to be the worst and potentially most dangerous president we have ever had. He has been the poster child for "Moral Superiority," the philosophy that whatever actions need to be taken to achieve an agenda validating it with the claim, it has "Good Intentions." He has been given many chances to make his actions match his words and each time has spectacularly failed to do so. He's not the common man he claims to be, but the ultimate imperial elitist. The president is and his staff have been the worst perpetrators of the "Class Warfare," that they allege to despise.

Chapter **FOUR**

<u>ALL OUR HEROES ARE DEAD</u>
<u>(AND MAYBE THEY SHOULD BE!!)</u>

Our sense of civility is a little preposterous of properly studied.

We have given our Hollywood elite - Actors, athletes and musicians - as much clout as the politicians. All of them are protective of each other, if given any critical analysis then you face the real possibility of being ostracized by their peers. If we give these people a pass from a critical eye, than we run the risk of having history repeated and all because they don't want to be remembered as being the bad guy, or even a flawed human being.

Untouchable Presidents

Everyone has skeletons in their closets, stupid or culturally bizarre actions. In the case of people from the past it might have been actions that were normal or acceptable in their time, but reviled by later generations. United States presidents are no exception, but for years they were treated as they were.

This has led to a movement by those who desire to denigrate our country (from within as well as from the outside) to spread what is unfettered truth, using these great men's eccentricities as reasons to minimalize their accomplishments or even vilify them in the court of public opinion. In other words, by putting them on so high a pedestal - without reminding the public they were mere mortals capable of error as the rest of us - we have put a target on their back by those with delusions of grandeur.

George Washington said to have had the teeth pulled from one of his slaves to use to fashion his own. Abraham Lincoln was reported to sleep in the same bed as men.

Not to advocate Washington's actions, aren't they a reflection of the nation's feelings of the times? Slaves were considered beasts of burden, same as the oxen or horse and were treated with the same regard even by those who advocated for their freedom.

With Lincoln this was a not uncommon custom of the time. These were not random men, but those who he knew quite well and was most comfortable with their company. Mostly ignored by those who repeat this is that it was not a sexual act.

More to the point, do these odd personal habits diminish what they did? Shouldn't we be judging the manner in which they governed, more than their personal lives? Shouldn't we be vetting George Washington about signing *Jay's* treaty? Or Lincoln about why he overstepped his authority with the railroad industry?

The other side of this is our propensity to ignore such faults of those we admire. How many democrats were eager to brush aside Clinton's martial affairs? Or republicans ignoring Newt Gingrich's affair? Whenever it's someone we agree with we dismiss such actions and move on, but if our contrarians did so we would be asking for their heads. Maybe we need to start looking as closely to those we respect as well.

Maybe we also need to remember all these people are as fallible as the rest of us, and focus on whether they are looking out for those they serve. In the end that's the most important part and the rest is smoke and mirrors.

Role Models are Humans too

When people go on and on about how disappointed and how disillusioned they feel when they hear of scandals involving their favorite sports figures, an actor or other celebrity, I feel kind of bad. Mostly for the one who is complaining, maybe it's just me but I don't really even care that much what these people do.

They are human, they falter like the rest of us. The only real difference is the tabloid media focuses so heavily on them. Why do we as our society hold our celebrities to a higher level than the rest of us? Because they are talented in film or television, or they can hit the ball the farthest? Why does the fact they are in the limelight mean that they shouldn't live in the manner that suits them best?

The best course of action is to tell people to try not to emulate them in their personal lives. The media rewards them with more exposure, for the worst behavior after all. So why is it surprising that they do the things they do? With our culture looking for them to slip and fall, what kind of parent would want their children to act like Johnny Depp? With the incentive being reward for bad behavior, why would you want your children to be little Miley Cyrus clones?

I'm not begrudging the celebrities their right to live their lives, if they want to do stupid stuff that's on them - but if you find it objectionable let your kids know. You might not be able to shelter them from it; but they should know how you feel about it.

Be your own Hero

Why do we rely on role models so much? It doesn't make sense. All a role model does is hold you back really. You focus too much on doing things the way your role model would do things and you lose a part of yourself. We put too much faith in "superman."

We shouldn't embrace this "superman, will you save us" tendency - looking for the lone hero to come to restore law and order - but instead cultivate the mentality to come with solutions yourself or with the help of the community. Maybe superman hasn't really helped the people but enabled them.

Angelina Jolie: Modern Joan of Arc?

The actress Angelina Jolie was informed that she might get breast cancer because it runs in her family and that does increase your chances of getting it. So she does what any normal woman would do- she cried, cursed, pleaded with God (or whatever her deity choice is, I have no idea what the woman believes in) and has her breasts removed... Wait... What?

Actually all but that last part is quite normal and healthy, but getting a major surgery because of a *possibility* of a health malady is absurd! It's like getting Chemotherapy treatment, just to be sure. It's one thing to do what you can to prevent it from occurring or exhausting all other options to save your

79

life after being diagnosed - but having a major surgery to remove a part of your body because of a possibility? Can you say reactionary?

Look, I really don't care what she does to herself, that's her business and not mine, but this praising her, saying how brave she is for making such a huge sacrifice is a dangerous precedence. This was a very difficult decision I'm sure, but going under the knife for something she still has a chance not to have (I know I'm harping on that point, but I really want it to sink in on how stupid it is) - is an ill-advised risk.

This should not be touted up as a heroic act; someone who goes through cancer is far more heroic. The one who goes through surgery without a present danger is hardly heroic. Angelina is not the only woman to do this either, one of the Miss America Pageant contestants was reported to have had her breast removed as well, I was so glad she didn't win! Only because there would have been this looming question - did she win because she actually deserved it, or because of this stunt. The point is these are not actions to hold up for high praise, these are scared women taking unnecessary risks, which in doing so is a slap in face of those who have survived cancer. If anyone is the hero in this it's those who have beaten the odds, not those who jumped ship before they even knew the boat was sinking.

Unsung Heroes Part 1: Parents

Parents have always been the ones responsible for their children - making sure they know what is needed to function in society, that's a piece of wisdom that I never thought had to be stated as anything except the obvious. With the recent shift of cultural responsibility this is no longer the case!

The effect of the parents influence on children is being minimized by the pop culture elites. Remember the statement in the MSNBC ad - *"people think of their children as theirs, but they belong to the whole community."*

I see, so the whole community gave birth to the child; the whole community was involved in the conception; the community was there to teach them to ride their first bikes; or read to them at night and tuck them in.

This kingdom of stupidity that we have to deal with is from these hard-core elitists. Now it's not enough that they think they know what's best for the adult populace, but that they know what's best for your children. Oh the arrogance.

Unsung Heroes Part 2: Teachers

There are some amazing teachers out there who love what they do and are good at what they do. The tragedy is that we will never know because of all the inept ones who get a free pass, through the tenure program.

Tenure is one of the worst ideas every dreamt up by the "they know better" educated status quo proponents. It rewards the educators who show up for the paycheck and punishes the others who actually have ideas that will reach children to get them to enjoy learning and school.

But this is the world of government schools, where you're indoctrinated and taught what you're supposed to know rather than how to come to conclusions on your own. This structure of learning not only is immoral and inefficient, but makes children hate school.

Go ask the children out of government versus a charter school, which one is more enjoyable. In the charter schools the kids love school! Really! They're more excited to be there and learn. We are propagandized by the teachers unions, the NEA and the teachers themselves, that we must protect public schools or the children will suffer. There's no accountability with government schools, the reason for the lack of proficiency. That should be no surprise though; it is a government service after all.

Unsung Heroes Part 3: Capitalists

Capitalists are all greedy and only look out for themselves, that a prevailing sentiment in America, but are they really the bad guy? Is their drive of self-interest really a bad thing?

For the most part we all are looking out for our own best interest, but these captains of industry have money and prestige, so we are suspicious of how they got there. Who did they cheat to get there? Who did they scam?

Despite what popular culture wants you to believe, most of them are honest and hard workers. This skepticism is a push of envy and jealousy, by those who wish to keep the country divided to gain power and control. But in the end the capitalists are not the villain, but deserve our *praise* - they are the ones who bring us the helpful products we have today.

They make not only the mousetraps, but make the mousetraps better. They make everything in our lives better. We all work at our jobs for money, even if we also do it because it helps others, that's an added bonus - but the main reason is money same as the capitalists. How are the rest of us any better than the capitalists that are so despised? Other than the level of their success, I mean. We're not and that's the point, we have no reason to be mad at those who have succeeded and we should be looking at things their way - how can I make that product better? Then we can all be heroes.

Eminem likes it, So Should You

The fixation with Eminem has me more than a little baffled. It's not the typical demographic that listen to him either - take *New York Times* columnist, Maureen Dowd.

Dowd is not a stupid person by any means, but she and her girlfriends are enamored with him, to quote one of her columns -

"A gaggle of my girlfriends are surreptitiously smitten with Eminem. They buy his posters on eBay. They play him on their Walkmen at the gym."

Why do they worship at the cult of Eminem? Is it because he's an anomaly, a white rapper? Of all the white trash that has tried their hands at rap music, none have been as successful.

It could be because he is so angry, even more than most in his field and angry liberals gravitate towards other liberals like a magnet.

Hero today, Villain tomorrow

Almost thirty years ago celebrity chef and democrat, Paula Dean made controversial racially-charged statements - fast forward to the year 2013, she was hanged in the court of public opinion.

There are two points I want to get out in front in this segment before going into my analysis. First, it should be noted I don't care for Paula Dean - her politics or her personality. She's a loud, obnoxious, liberal woman, who in my opinion is more than a little insane. So, it would seem a bit of a paradox for me to defend her and my argument did confuse some who read my original article *"The Execution of Paula Dean."*

I don't know what Dean had said that had people fired up and if the stores that covered her products felt it was the right course of action to pull them, that's their choice - that doesn't mean I agree with them. That was my point, their disturbing reactionaryism in the face of comments made twenty-seven years ago was wrong.

Dean is not the only liberal who has had to deal with this either, actor Tim Allen, had his run in with the P.C. witch hunt crowd.

This kind of extraction of those who have the gall to have an independent thought - deviation from the democratic common consensus can't be allowed. But this is nothing new and many who have made comments against the actions of the party of leaders have been shunned, but for it to be after twenty-seven years seemed rather… petty.

It makes one wonder if maybe Dean might have committed a worse transgression, but with how fickle people can be towards those with different positions on issues it's hard to say for sure.

Doctors aren't so bad, Just Healthcare is

As with most advocates of socialism they have to sell it anyway they can and one of the best ways is to offer the people essentially what amounts to bribes. That's what entitlements are and you can't discuss entitlements without healthcare.

One the most absurd arguments is saying that healthcare is a "right." No it's not, it's a service and product.

The costs of healthcare are what makes it an easy sell, but like so many times these socialists have to ignore one piece of logic - the government sets the rules, so how does giving them *even more* power when they don't make things better with the power they already have? They ignore it because it goes against their cause. So, instead they deflect the blame onto the actors in the capitalist system, insurance companies and the doctors.

It's easy to blame the insurance companies I used to as well, but for most people the insurance system works as is. Those who have prediagnosed conditions are excluded because it would cost everyone more and since they didn't already pay into the system they are technically scamming the system.

The doctors went through a lot of schooling and it's very expensive, unless they are in a hospital setting they have to buy very expensive equipment. The doctors who drive the expensive cars I'm sure are the ones that work at the hospitals and not the private practitioners. These are the ones that will go out of business, with the Affordable Care Act.

With "free" insurance we will have massive lines with people flooding the hospitals for a cold instead of legitimate health issues. It's happened in basically every country that switched to socialized medicine. Canada is always held up as the model for socialized medicine, but in that country it's still not the doctors at the hospitals that give the best care there, not the legal ones at least.

Spread out across the country there are clinics that have left the mainstream socialized healthcare system, and have set up black market clinics. In their country the black market clinics are the ones with the best doctors of their country and who offer the superior care. With socialized medicine the black market clinics are the sterile, clean places with the top of the line equipment and lower prices. The black market there is a free market, so they can and do compete, not held hostage by the government regulations.

That's why we should be exploring *Health Savings Accounts*. Your employer offers a certain amount within an account and whatever you don't use gets saved for you. You have to pay more into it but it works. When they have a HSA the employees shop around for the best deals and voluntarily adopt preventative treatments.

But maybe the all-time best option is not dealing with insurance at all. Not taking insurance means that doctors don't have to hire people to navigate through the insurance paperwork and they get to focus on patient care.

Doctors under this model also tend to be more generous with their time for their patients and might try to help you find less expensive alternatives to the expensive drugs or even the alternative medical treatments, such as chiropractor services, acupuncture or massage therapy. You receive better treatment because of a more personal relationship, which under the Affordable Care Act you will treated as another number.

In Canada the best doctors are the Veterinarians, because they don't have the red tape and are not included in socialized medicine. Prices drop for the care and quality of care increases with less government involved. We should be protesting for *less* government in healthcare, not more.

Chapter **FIVE**

OVERPOPULATION: PROBLEM OR SOLUTION

There are a lot of very odd theories that have been advanced by different propagandists in the green communities. Overpopulation is the foundation for the agenda.

This chapter will go into the environmental conventional wisdom storyline.

Fitting **together nicely** like a jigsaw puzzle, the overpopulation movement has utilized the government green and pro-abortion agendas seamlessly. As far as I'm concerned the pro-choice issue is the doctor patient privilege and not a federal one - the partial birth abortion is a completely different situation. This is the debate for me - pro-choice vs. pro-entitlement and pro-partial birth abortion.

The confusion the general public has with the libertarian philosophy in this is that those that are pro-choice are pro-abortion, that's simply not the case. Basically we don't want the federal government to make a stance for or against, if they get involved at *all* I would say its role would be to monitor the facilities performing the procedures to make sure safety and sanitation concerns are observed - but even that could be and should be, done by the private sector.

Okay, back to the Partial Birth Abortion part of this segment, this is one of the few issues where a little emotion needs to be injected into the discussion. Now for those who are sensitive to this issue and don't want to lose your lunch, during the next part of this segment I do include a description of the procedure, if you want to avoid it, it's in italics.

One of the key figures in the partial birth

abortion movement is Dr. Martin Haskell the man who pioneered the procedure, the technical term he coined was "dilation and extraction" or D and E.

The killing of a fully formed, prehuman being, accomplished by the insertion of scissors into the base of the head and using a suction machine the brain is removed.

He devised the D and E procedure in 1992 and the doctor has performed it thousands of times and admits to that. In a 1993 interview in *Cincinnati Medicine*, Dr. Haskell stated, *"I noticed that some of the later D and E's were very, very easy. So I asked why can't they all happen this way. You see [with] the easy ones... you'd reach up and grab the foot of the fetus, pull the fetus down and the head would hang up and then you would collapse the head and take it out. It was easy.*

"At first, I would reach around trying to identify a lower extremity [a foot] blindly with the tip of my instrument. I'd get it right about 30-50% of the time. Then I said 'Well gee, if I put the ultrasound up there I could see it all and wouldn't have to feel around for it."

The partial birth abortion issue is a clear-cut case of infanticide! This is indisputable and an active attempt by a medical professional to act on the most innocent of human beings in a manner similar to the occupants of *Auschwitz*.

    As disturbing as it is to the ones who go

through the D and E's were actually the lucky ones, there suffering was fairly short lived, many have died from exposure. Dr. Ron Paul has told about the way the medical field used to do abortions in the seventies, which was to remove the child, place the child in the corner of the room and let it die. I'm sorry, but I would rather give the doctor the green light to inject the child with a fatal dose of morphine, it would be better than callously let it suffer - that would be the more humane choice.

Dr. Paul is an active anti-abortion crusader, but even he doesn't want this to be a government issue, same as most pro-life libertarians, I would think.

I titled this segment, *Modern Eugenics* and I'm getting to that. Eugenics, is the active move to create the perfect human. The Nazis did it with their Aryan nation policies including the Holocaust and the primitive steps in genetic manipulation, if the regime had lasted another ten or fifteen years, that dream of the "perfect race" in Nazi Germany may have become a horrible reality.

In modern times that's the reality here in America, thanks to the partial birth abortion movement. After the term of about six months, birth defects such as spina bifida or Down's syndrome can be detected, this is when a lot of women request the procedure. Coincidence? No, it's not at all.

The women here have opted to kill these children rather than have an "imperfect" child. What's wrong with putting the child up for adoption? At this stage the child is able to survive with help of doctors, instead because of partial birth abortion the nation has turned the family doctor into Dr. Mengele.

This is about depopulating the United States, down to a "manageable" population that Henry Kissinger warned us about. Barack Obama, as a senator had a chance to make partial birth abortion illegal in Illinois and didn't, because he believed that one restriction on abortion would be call for a full prohibition of it. That's a reasonable conclusion.

There are times that early term abortions are necessary, where health complications of the mother would put both at risk. Or if the soon to be child put the mother at severe risk. Or the mother was a victim of rape or incest, she should not have to suffer carrying and having the child.

Restrictions proposed by some of the virtuous absolutists would infringe on at times necessary, although be it unpleasant, medical procedures. So, then we have the argument that we have to have contraceptives and abortion paid for, for low income families. Under ObamaCare there is going to be an additional 115,000 federally funded abortions. Many of these families are low income because they choose to be, they already take federal assistance which kills ambition. Less government fix this, not more of it. The choices we are given with it being in the hands of government - either, unfettered, unrestricted and abused medical procedures that are paid for by those who find the practice aberrant, or restrictions on medical personnel who at times need to make the tough call to save the life that can be saved. Seeing now fouled up things get with government involvement that should be the first thing aborted here.

Modern Eugenics Part 2:
Another problem

There's an argument by some very smart people that because the world is such a horrible place that bringing children into it is an act of inhumanity. "How can I bring a child into this world?"- they argue. So they don't and only the stupid will breed. It sounds like a sick joke, but it's not.

Through a carefully designed and maintained system of propaganda by special interest groups espousing the theory of *Overpopulation,* this argument is a godsend. Across the world populations are down and continue to fall. Some countries are already having varied social problems from it. Mostly it's because with improved medical services their older generations won't do their civic duty and die!

Our country is going into this phase and guess who's going to suffer the most? That's right, the elderly. Right now it's looking like the baby boomers that will suffer the brunt of it.

In the future the United States will not have a predictable population, so let's bring in more immigrants to fix the problem. That will solve it right? Even with that we are in trouble. We need the population to double to have a sustainable population again.

So what has been the cause of this? The biggest factor is the economy really. People don't want to have children when the fiscal outlook is

93

shaky. To be fair that is commendable, waiting for financial stability is responsible especially for those in the lower incomes bracket. For those who can afford it though, for the sake of the country it's your responsibility to procreate. For those who can't afford to have kids, who can work but choose not to, get back to work. Your country needs you to have kids, so go do.

As for the notion, "how can I bring children into this world?"- bring them into this world to fix it. We are running out of smart people and need their help.

Green Oppression

There is this odd activism trifecta correlation between modern eugenics, overpopulation and the green movement. Overpopulation and the modern eugenics system are tied together with their push for Partial Birth Abortion, but how does the green movement tie into all this?

Mostly because the theory is the more people there are the more resources that will be consumed and the greenhouse gasses will spike, but that hasn't been the end result.

For one thing, the market has voluntarily changed their practices to be more environmentally friendly and then made sure to advertise it to the general public, which is why they did it but the point is they already did it themselves.

My contention in the green discussions is the deficiency of correlation with the cause and effect that climate scientists have not been able to prove - and the claims they have made already been proven false.

They claimed by 2012, we would have massive floods, caused by the arctic icecaps melting; they claimed we are in a state of global warming; and that the polar bear would be at a high risk of extinction. They didn't get even one of those right!

Not only are we not losing the icecaps - they are 60% *larger*, with millions of miles of ice growth that the climate scientists can't explain. *We are at a thirty year high in arctic ice growth.* We do have excess carbon emissions, but they have not had the traumatic effects predicted - satellite footage has shown an increase in global plant growth, you know nature's air filtration system!

Al Gore made his claim for restraint of fossil fuel consumption on the death of the polar bears - saying that they are an endangered species and will soon be extinct if we don't act now. Are they really endangered? I don't know, I'm sure the former vice president doesn't know either, because the people who are supposed to know have no idea how many there are. No one knows for sure if there are 1,000 or 100,000, they are guessing.

Everything about the green movement is based on speculation instead of hard science. The argument isn't are we having an effect on the planet, but how big of an effect? It can't be answered, no one knows and they can't show a direct connection to our actions and climate change, the examples given of cause but can't prove effect.

During the 1970's, the climate scientists changed their minds and said that the earth is in a state of global cooling, with their new data they may be revising it again to global cooling, as the 700 scientists who said we are not in a stage of global warming. With all this guessing by the "experts" how can we trust a single word they say? Even John Kerry hasn't flip-flopped this much!

Let's buy a Prius

One of the biggest waste programs of a government policy was the "Cash for Clunkers" program. It was massively expensive that had an ambiguous outcome and was nothing more than a push of the hybrid car market.

Oh where to begin? If hybrids were such a good thing, why did they need federal assistance? That's easy, because it's a cornerstone of the "go green" government movement; that absurd heavy-handed eco-friendly federalism! Get more hybrids on the roads and lower CO_2 emissions, but it was a bad program that wasn't even thought all the way through. Imagine that, a government program that was expensive and inefficient, who would have guessed?

This is a program that would have worked

better if they had resold the cars, but it should have been done by the private sector market anyway. The private companies are already there and all the "Cash for Clunkers" did was hurt them.

It also took away a lot of "first cars" from the new drivers. The inexpensive fixer-uppers that can be beaten up and keep on going until the transmission falls out. Those old cars are a work of art too and treating them like that is the same as drawing a mustache on the Mona Lisa.

They should have been taken to the custom shops, where they could have been fixed up to their former glory and not completely scrapped for no other reason than to appease a flawed ideology by a group of moronic activists. Most government programs are just a waste of money, this one is also a waste of amazing pieces of machinery as well, it's very sad.

Spaceship Earth: Where it all began

Since the beginning of civilization and the development of the moral code, the intellectuals of every era - Aristotle for an example - have pondered the effect of our growing population on this planet.

Will we decimate the natural resources beyond the sustainable limits? What do our wars and other actions have - as far as their lasting outcomes - on the planet and its other inhabitants? These are legitimate concerns, but the science and its conclusions in the modern age are - questionable. Let's take a look at one of the more prevailing theories, the *Spaceship Earth*.

I'm sorry, but even the name of this theory is dumb! Spaceship Earth - are you kidding? It sounds like a transvestite lounge in New Orleans and during Madre Gras every night is "ladies night." But the simplicity of it is intentional, it's meant to be part of the academic curriculum aimed at grade schools children. That's what the framers even state, as the earth being the same as a spaceship - a closed system with limited resources that aren't renewable and that the overpopulation of the planet by our species will lead to an environmental cataclysm.

What makes all this so dangerous is that its proponents have a plan to solve it... sterilizations. *"First, it will be on a voluntary basis, but if needs be by force,"* said one of the movements proponents. All the green movement is junk science used to advance scary prospects. Good to see the enviro's have left the emotional absolutism at the door.

The ELFS are not Happy

The ELF group has gone through a lot of changes in the past couple of decades; its origins are reported to have started out as the *Environmental Life Force* during the seventies and now is the *Earth Liberation Front*, founded by the heads of the original *ELF* movement and *Earth First!*

They have ties to the Animal Liberation Front and in cooperation they have caused billions of dollars' worth of damage across California, Oregon and Washington and parts of Canada.

The group doesn't consider the loss of property as important or illegal, as this statement posted anonymously on their webpage clearly expresses:

"This isn't terrorism-domestic, eco, or otherwise. Its property damage aka arson. The perps may be misguided, but so are the people who buy such big houses and builders who cater to that segment of the market."

The group touts up the fact that there haven't been any deaths from their actions; the *FBI* had this to say, that "…We're lucky. Once you start one of these fires they can go way out of control." The FBI takes this very seriously, as they should and had named ELF the largest most active US based terrorist group of 2001 and 2002.

The organization must be reaching others though, unfortunately, since the movie based on the life of one of its members was up for awards in 2011. The documentary titled *If a tree falls*, is about ELF member Daniel McGowan and the two fire bombings in Eugene, Oregon that landed him and his accomplices in prison.

Besides, these zealots are ignoring the fact that destruction of property is illegal and destruction of property is still harming others - their actions hurt the environment as well. How much carbon do they think goes into the environment from these fires? That's not including the accelerants used. This is my major contention with these idiot activists, they let their emotions dictate their actions and don't think them through. They don't even think about the ramifications to what they are trying to protect - which goes to show they care more about making the statement than the issue they claim to espouse.

Other eco-terrorists

Probably the most biased environmental groups is the one that claims it's not: the *Intergovernmental Panel on Climate Change*. It was founded in 1988 with the conjuncture of the government organizations - the *World Meteorological Organization* and the *United Nations Environmental Programme*, later to be endorsed by the *United Nations* General Assembly.

The mission of the IPCC is to provide assessments of scientific data about the risks of climate change by mankind and come up with solutions for minimizing the effects of human's influence. It's through a voluntary basis and the scientists on the panel are not being paid by the IPCC, it should be noted that the data is not their own, and they are merely reporting what others have done and postulating about the outcome.

This organization is the complete brainchild and slave to the *United Nations*, which would explain its inefficiencies and why its conclusions should be viewed with a dubious eye.

Windmills aren't all that blows

Many would probably claim I'm against the alternative energies market, that's not the case at all! It's an innovative market that has great potential, not only to reduce green-house gases but to save the consumer money by bringing competition into the energy market.

Alternative energies are not a bad thing at all - the federal intrusion into it, that's what's detrimental. The government has taken a market that doesn't need help to function and flourish and is holding it prisoner as a means to control the energy market. That's one of the tools to control a society - along with censorship of literature or other forms of information, and education.

It's been reported that the energy market is scared of the alternative energy boom and they should be. Not because of the competition, but because of the regulations. The federalized energy monopoly won't put up with having others in their cash crop. The energy companies not in on the scam should be afraid of that.

There are serious reservations I have about wind and other alternative fuels. The objection to alternative fuels themselves is if it's made from a food staple it inflates the price of that product in stores, that's a bigger problem. Look at corn, since the introduction of corn ethanol the American families have seen a jump of $2,000 a year at the grocery store, from corn-based products and meats from animals that graze on corn.

Wind is one of the oldest forms of energy, but if it's so great, why doesn't it get used more? It's loud, inefficient and the turbines are eyesores. When windmills were proposed to be placed near the Kennedy compound, uber-environmentalist Ted Kennedy flipped. Even hard-core environmentalists don't want these fixtures in their backyards. The contention over alternative energy has more to do with the government than the introduction of options, after all, when the feds get involved in a market - *then* it does become a monopoly.

Getting out of the Fracking Business

Fracking is a technique of getting natural resources out of the earth in a manner that causes minimal environmental damage. Advocates for it report that natural gas is the resource that they aim for, it burns cleaner and has been discovered in hundreds of gallons - if processed and refined not only could the United States be completely self-sufficient, but we could be selling to other nations.

With all this everyone should be happy, but they're not. Because of environmental groups, a lot of people have been protesting fracking... Why? What are their concerns? The documentary *Gasland* is the answer to that - this film has propagandized the reports of fires from the water taps and linked it to natural gas contaminating the water through fracking.

The film makers didn't do their research before making this speculation though, but the counter film, *Fracknation* did and what they discovered was very interesting.

To start off with the gases that cause tap water to ignite is not limited to the areas where fracking is done - but in tap water across the country. That doesn't mean water from fracking is not contaminated, there could still be run-off in some cases. Not according to the EPA, at the examples in *Gasland*, the local chapters of the EPA tested the tap water of the families of the film.

The results were zero contaminates - the family was surprisingly less than thrilled. Fuming, they ordered the EPA agents out of their house, despite the fact *they* requested the test - they didn't handle the loss of their pay-out very well, and basically called them incompetent. One family from *Gasland* when approached for comment by the *Fracknation* film crew, called the cops saying they were being "harassed." Since when is an interview "harassment?" All you have to do is say no to the interview. It goes to show that every once in while the EPA does do a good thing.

Chapter **SIX**

SOCIAL IDIOCY

The title heading says it all. The smartest animal on the planet, doing the dumbest things, for the most moronic of reasons.

The End of Oil... Not Bloody Likely

The oil industry has been getting a lot of bad press, but is it valid? Not really, many have contention with it because environmentalists have engrained into us that we should be against them.

They say not only we should abandon oil, but we could. Are they right? Is it even possible to get away from oil? The answer to that is a most definite - No! What they want you think is that we only use oil in our cars and in industry. That's not even close to being true; we use it in multiple products. Some will even surprise you!

Everything uses oil somehow. Roads, electronics, even food and sunscreen. Most of our sunscreen is from refined industrial oil, between 80-90% to be more precise.

We even ingest products made of oil - aspirin for one. That's just for starters, other uses of oil includes - it's use to make lipstick, shoes, clothing and products to clean the clothes. It's used in toothpaste, shaving cream, soaps, hand lotions, candles, soft contact lenses, dice, movie film, artificial turf, crayons and antifreeze.

It's also used in Medical fields as well, for heart valves, denture adhesives, cortisone and antihistamines. It's also used in food preservatives, vitamin capsules, curtains, lubricants, waxes, inks, solvents, floor wax, caulking, ammonia and guitar strings.

In pretty much every possible market we use oil and this list is a small sampling of how we use oil, and coal is the same way - about 20% of our society depends on the coal industry. To claim that we can go without oil or coal goes up in smoke.

Voluntary Segregation

One of the most heated topics in global politics is the debate on Multiculturalism and most of the contention comes from its ambiguous definition and it's being misused in conversation.

Multiculturalism is a societal structure that is a mixture of different races and cultures, a melting pot - which is what America has always been and should continue to be. Almost every American citizen has taken advantage of this - because without multiculturalism there would be no America, plain and simple. The debate gets tricky, because the terms, *Naturalization* and *Assimilation* are tied in and shouldn't be, those are separate issues.

Multiculturalism is about immigrants expressing themselves, individuality and should be embraced, not infringed upon, individuality is the cure for these problems because the individual can come up with solutions to the problems from Naturalization and Assimilation - which is what causes the division and *Voluntary Segregation*.

That's not to say that we should tolerate

violent behavior, even if it's a part of their culture, but if we lump together those that adhere to their cultural violence with those who are part of that culture but doesn't practice the violent rituals, we will have unnecessarily alienated the peaceful immigrant. In this country there are *Natural Laws* that should be adhered to - murder, destruction of property or theft, are all universally wrong and must be adhered to, but to keep people from celebrating their cultural heritage is just as unethical, as well.

It's no different from the secularists' war with Christmas or the moralists fight against Halloween. When we create a hostile environment with blanket legislature that penalizes those who are simply trying to express themselves, they will lash out, the same way those who are reading this fight against government intrusion in our lives.

If they are American citizens they have as much a right to express themselves as the rest of us.

What did you Say

While the diversity of cultures and traditions has proven beneficial to the country, there is a major negative factor to it as well, and that is from the inaction of English language beeing declared the official language of the United States and it has created extreme contention in the country. This has, in fact, been the greatest influence of division in the multiculturalism debate and the reason is clear - it doesn't matter how brilliant your solution is, if it can't be expressed to others.

Critics of the call for English declared the official language claim that it minimizes other ethnic cultures by eliminating their language and putting the American culture above their own. This is simply not true. That's absurd, mostly because America is a homogenous mix of all cultures; and the culture of their origin is already integrated into it. Another point to consider, almost every nation has adopted modern English as part of their society to do business in the global economy. Our nation is the only developed country to take exception to this push - being probably the only nation not to have an official language.

The thing is, just because we name an official language, doesn't take away the rich significance of the other cultures of the world, or diminish their impact; or force them to abandon their native cultures, to standards designated by others that would be unethical and unconstitutional. What this is a call for, is to make it easier for interactions to occur within our society, without confusion; so the salesperson doesn't have to learn another language to do their job, or so multiple languages don't have to be posted on our products - both of which adds additional cost to enterprise.

Lastly, the greatest justification for it is that it encourages the integration of the multiple ethnic groups. In prisons and poor parts of the country they don't intermingle with other ethnicities, keeping to "their own kind" saying it's acceptable to not adopt the language and the nation's general sentimentalities

- this attitude continues ethnic division. Not letting others be themselves is part of the *multiculturalism* dilemma, but not assimilating into the culture at all is the other.

Well, I'm from New York!

It's hilarious in T.V. shows to watch when someone from the big apple goes into the unknown of nature, because they all have use those same reassuring words - I'll be fine. After all, I'm from New York!

Whether they are talking to themselves to try to sum up courage, or to a loved one so racked with anxiety about them going into an alien world, that's the way they always deal with it. Like saying this magical phrase is going to impress a hoard of guerrilla mercenaries of Korea or insurgents of the Middle East. Try saying that to one of the local wildlife and see how far that will get you. Most people would jump to the conclusion that bears, alligators, and wolves would be the only animals to be worried about... they would be wrong! That's how people get hurt all the time in the National Parks; they avoid the large predators, but not the grazers, the buffalo, deer and moose that appear docile and approachable.

Consider that for a moment though. This is a large animal, that's very survival is based on it's either running or charging a predator. What are the chances of it deciding to attack rather than to flee? What signs do you look for? Apparently, others have not given that much thought either. According to reports more people are attacked by deer than bears. The highest numbers of deaths in the U.S. are by the smallest animals. It's actually insects, ants, bees, and spiders. In some areas, that accounts for the greater percentage of deaths by wildlife. The largest number of deaths globally, is by the mosquito.

The numbers and type of animals that cause this vary by the variety and proximity to civilization though. Snakes and spiders are the greatest killers in Australia, but the kangaroo, the red and grey, specifically are also very dangerous. Their defensive weapons: Massive powerful legs. They can balance all their weight on their tails, to maximize the blow. As if that's not enough, on the ends of their feet are two inch, razor sharp claws. It's not a surprise for someone to get fatally wounded, or even disemboweled by a single kick.

This attitude about predators being so unseemly is rather odd if you really think about it. Our species eats meat, yet we are quick to judge our fellow predators of the animal kingdom. It goes a step further though; some psychologists believe that our innate fear is where our creation of dragons was born. It was hard-wired fear our primate fore-bearers had of these apex predators.

Legal Scammers

Pick a card, any card. You do and the magician will end up showing you the card you picked. Wow! How does he do it? Don't know, don't care. Sit back and enjoy the show and don't focus on it. His occupational title is "illusionist", for a reason, he's admitting he's going to con you.

There are unscrupulous individuals that will take this to the next level and use it to their financial gain, using cons that shouldn't work but do. The biggest con-artists aren't the street performers, however, but by the Federal Reserve through a flawed monetary policy.

When Mitt Romney was campaigning for president in 2012 he said he considered China a "currency manipulator", but how is the American financial system any better? Isn't our system of monetary policy about "currency manipulation?"

The end result of being taken off the gold standard, quantative easing and the devaluation of the dollar by mass printing isn't that "currency manipulation?" The end result of all of this is the American people suffer most and the dollar is basically a worthless piece of paper. The only reason our country isn't in worse economic trouble is that so many of the other countries adopted the euro.

Out of the choice of being swindled by the conman or the government, I think I prefer the conman, at least he knows when to walk away.

Do Something!

Remember those old black and white horror movies, the ones that when something happened the villagers all ran home to get their torches, pitchforks or shotguns and then go to their governor or other representative to take care of the problem. Mob rule was their form of justice and the hotter heads prevailed, that was just a movie though it doesn't really happen - does it? Actually it happens all the time and here in America as well.

Rather than let an investigation find out what the real cause is of the tragedy, it gets blown out of proportion into a National Emergency. Most of the time it's not a national emergency, however, but an isolated incident. Our turning it into a national emergency is what makes it one. Look at the attention that has been given to school shootings, the perpetrators "15 minutes of fame" lasts for months! Remember people want to matter; it's irrelevant whether it's for saving a couple from a burning building or shooting up a movie theater.

The incentive for prolonged attention seekers is obviously skewed in favor of the villain, so why act in a manner that will benefit society? That's the message that is being sent out anyway.

So why does the governor so eagerly fan the flames of public anger? In part it's to be reelected, but that's not the *main* goal. See, what they don't show in the movies is the scariest part - the governor does it so he can pass more laws, laws designed to take away more of your freedoms while promising more security. He's using the *State of Emergency*, because he knows that with your emotions their highest peak you're not thinking clearly and when that does fade, it's either too late or something else will happen that he can use to convince you his actions are "for your own good." If it was really "for your own good" he wouldn't have to sell it to you.

Government Showdown

The government and its lapdog media are good at whipping the complacent public into a frenzy, even when it's about nothing. Only 17% of the government was "shut down", 17% that's nothing and a good share of it wasn't a genuine "cut" since the federal employees were reimbursed for their "lost" wages.

Not surprising were the agencies that weren't on the list - big spending organizations like the EPA or IRS, also not on the list were the military, they were on active duty and got paid for their service. *Social Security,* Medicare and Medicaid recipients also still got their benefits.

About 1,350,000 "essential" (whatever the hell that means) federal employees continued to get paid during the "shutdown" and 100,000,000 government checks were cashed during this farce.

With exceptions of the National Parks, Veterans Memorials and the customer service positions associated with the before mentioned places, the "shutdown" seemed rather anemic.

If they want to see a *real* government shut down, vote in a libertarian president in the next election - see how many government agencies would no longer be in existence and replaced with privatized ones that are actually beneficial to everyone, including those utilizing the programs.

While I do feel sorry for those who were played as pawns in all this and agree it's unfair, the "shutdown" was nothing more than a political pissing contest - and it was the Republican establishment that blinked first, again.

I Won the Lottery, now Where's my Welfare Check

This is direct evidence that the federal government couldn't care less about getting a handle on the unfettered spending on welfare spending since the recession and the example set by the Obama administration. Lottery winners who don't see any problems with getting their welfare checks after their windfall.

The source of this attitude is not only the example set by the nation's leaders, but by the inactions by the government organizations to investigate and detain those abusing the system.

Now, I realize there are a lot of people on welfare and they can't get every one of them, but a part of their job is to monitor their illegibility for welfare. When the recipient gets an inheritance or lottery winnings, they are immediately disqualified for welfare.

This is a system that needs reform, but it needs to be altered to make it harder for those abusing the system, while protecting the recipients that are on it for valid reasons. With all the billions spent in entitlements there's not one analyst on staff? Not one person qualified to check for redundancies? If not then fire some "non-essential" employees in the IRS or the GSA. Maybe the same ones that made those stupid videos.

This is ridiculous that we, the taxpayers, are subsidizing those who can work and choose not to, but now those who hit the jackpot as well. When did the nation go from, "ask not what your country can do for you, but what you can do for your country", to "where's my welfare check."

Poverty this is Not

The newest "need" in the ever expanding list of federal bribes for the "free stuff" voters, has now included the X Box entitlement and the price is giving your eternal soul to the democrats.

So, let's see, there was already free healthcare, education, the "Obama-phones", even smart phones for enrolling in *ObamaCare*, food stamps and now an X Box, okay makes sense. What's next then? How about free cars? Or free houses? - Oh wait they have those already too, thanks to *HUD*.

How did we get to the point that so many in

this country don't even know what actual poverty is? Poverty is when you have to sell your blood to get your next meal. Or when you have to sell your car and ride a bike or the bus to work, because you couldn't make rent. Poverty is about making sacrifices for *real* necessities, like food, shelter, water, not a new $300.00 pair of sneakers or a new T.V.

Poverty is only temporary if you turn away from the shiny objects by Uncle Obama, if you give in you helped add another person to the unemployment line. These "free things" aren't free, maybe for you but others are paying for them.

If you're going on *SNAP* so you can buy liquor or lobster or steak, it's not being responsible and that's not poverty. Ever read about what life is like in the Middle East? How about in parts of Africa? Or Korea? Even go back a few decades in this country's history, poverty was a lot different. During the Great Depression luxury amenities was more like soup from a soup kitchen, not filet mignon, or a cot and blanket not the latest gadget.

The drunk living under the highway bridge, sleeping in his urine in America lives better than the affluent in other countries. He has enough money for his favorite spirit, usually can find food and a shelter.

Actually if you see him begging for money at the local grocery store, he might be doing alright, they can make a couple of hundred a day doing that.

Real poverty is not being behind everyone in the technological toys; it's about surviving and figuring out how to change your situation. Many of the most powerful men rose from nothing -

Rockefeller, Carnegie and Vanderbilt, or more contemporary figures like, Bill Gates and the late Steve Jobs. The claim of hardship should inspire you to be better, not enslave you to the ghettos. That's what the entitlement culture does though, it fosters the need of "more" without the work to achieve it. So, it leaves the masses always wanting just that - "more."

Shame-less

There was a report a couple of months ago that in some cities representatives of the food stamps program SNAP, were actually going out to enlist people for the program. Oh yes, that's just what we need *more* people on food stamps!

But even this wasn't enough; those who enroll have to feel good about becoming a leech to the economy, or least not feel bad about it anyway. It's okay to be on a program that is sucking hoards of money and ripe with abuse, from an already stagnant economy. It's okay not to contribute anything to society and be a weight on the honest hard-working middle class families.

Who cares about the middle class anyway? Obama said he did, but his actions speak loud and clear, in the "Obama-nomics" system it's only those in "poverty" that really matter.

One of the representatives of SNAP had the audacity to claim the nation was on the brink of "rampant hunger." What? Where? We are the most obese nation in the world! That's what the Health Gestapo has been saying, it sounds like the feds need to get together and get their stories straight. Is it rampant hunger or leader in obesity? Which lie will they go with?

Ship them off to Military School

Here's a social stigma that has always had muddled logic and I hope is more myth than truth!

Whenever a child acts up its suggested they should be shipped to Military School, now if they are an average "I need attention" or "Mommy and daddy didn't give me enough disciple so I wound up a spoiled selfish little pain in the ass"; that's one thing, but if they are a future Timothy McVeigh or they hold up Jack the Ripper as a role model, a sanatorium is a better choice than active duty.

If they have violent tendencies putting them in a social pressure cooker, with all the screaming; cursing commanding officers; drill sergeants with a God complex; training them to live for days on crickets; finding water and food in ways that would impress a doomsday prepper; and weapons training that can teach them to hit a fly at the other side of a football field, sending them to *West Point* might want to be reevaluated.

Call me crazy, but I think further encouraging

their predatory instincts will not be a boon to society, unless boon is short for boondoggle. It's like the argument of sending non-violent offenders to the same prison as rapists and mass murderers. Okay, let's teach them how to kill without caring, let's show them how to get away with lesser crimes before moving onto arson or murder, all by their prison bunkmate who murdered twenty people.

Both prison and the Military's purposes are not to kill the violent instincts, but to contain them and both rely on the willingness of the individual to work within the system or suffer. Those who show an unwillingness to contain these instincts should not be put in the field where their talents for pain and death will be utilized, but in a place where they will minimized. Those who can't be reformed in prison should be taken out of society for the good of its civilized citizenry and those who bashed in the heads of dogs and cats as children, should not be given a rifle.

Attack of the Googlemonster

When the story of the NSA data mining came out journalist and fellow libertarian John Stossel was, for once, not the first on the scene - but completely absent from the discussion. This had many in the libertarian circles buzzing - where was Stossel on this? Why was he not angry?

In an article he gave a two part reasoning, in

reply to angry and confused supporters - with the advent of Google and Facebook we have already lost all our privacy anyways, was the first part; the other argument was that we have legitimate threats to our country and data mining might be able to stop more violence. I'm not going to get into the second part of his comment, other than to say that Stossel is wrong on this and I agree with his detractors on it that his tolerance of the security state in the article is… well, puzzling - but the point about our loss of privacy is on par.

In the new documentary *Terms and Conditions May Apply,* this abandonment of the fourth amendment is thoroughly examined - showing the extremely disturbing ways the government agencies have used *Facebook* and *Twitter* to spy on us and intervene on legal activities of inconvenient protest and assembly.

It ends with a visit to the founder of Facebook, Mark Zuckerberg (they found his house using Google maps, by the way), to interview him - when he finally stepped out of his home and sees the camera he clams up, but when they turn off the handheld, he relaxes and even smiles. What Zuckerberg was unaware of was the interviewer had a camera built into his glasses and showed the country something he didn't mean to - his hypocrisy.

Zuckerberg and these internet moguls are the biggest hypocrites in the world; they guard their privacy vehemently but don't hesitate to intrude into ours. They think they are better and more deserving than those they really serve.

They think because they have come up with

an amazing product and have forgotten their customers use their product voluntarily, their first masters are the general public and not the United States government. Maybe the best way to remind them of this is to explore other options, or invent them, and bring their egos into check - that they are not as special as they might think.

Chapter SEVEN

LIBERALISM AMERICAN STYLE

Liberalism in America is so far from the original institution. It was created as a form of resistance from the monarchy in Europe, in this country it is the colluded effort of control by government and business. This is putting every facet of our lives in the hands of government.

Pseudo-humanitarianism in Action

In other countries liberalism in based on the theories of John Locke, who was critical of the crown and fought to have the power of the crown greatly lessen. Here in America, we have this bizarre, bastardized, progressive version that advocates the increase in power to the crown.

How did that happen? Is it because we have so much freedom, that the only way to rebel is to reign ourselves in? Regardless of the cause the problem is this system of propaganda. Those who are liberal use emotional arguments rather than logical ones to bring others into their ranks.

If their points were so valid though, why use such rhetoric for their cause? Why not be more forthcoming instead of employing emotional blackmail on the public? A lot of the time their representatives flat out lie to their constituency, but if their points are valid why resort to that? When there is a republican presidency, they claim to cut through the waste and get rid of inefficient social programs, they don't - but the Democrats claim they will. Why do the Democrats do this, say that republicans will leave you out in the cold? If they have the moral high ground why resort to such blatant fraud?

Instead they demonize anyone who disagrees with them. Even in the face of insurmountable evidence the American liberals cling to their oppressive ideals - guns are wrong, you should have a knife instead; we need more laws, more laws give us more freedom; animals have rights; people don't have to be accountable for themselves, because the government will look after them; sue those who disagree with you, they must be wrong and uneducated anyway; it's only okay to be against war if the man in the White House is a republican; individualism is wrong; and big business has created all our problems, government can fix it - even though they are the ones who created the bad laws to begin with.

So Mr. Liberal, I have to ask - How does making social programs that are not self-sufficient and can be canceled at any time, considered more humane? How does ignoring the people's objections to having tax dollars spent in ways they disagree with more humane? What ever happened to the Democratic Party that Andrew Jackson was so proud to call his own?

Bringing a Knife to Gunfight

One of the groups that I found on Facebook, called "*Americans against the Republican Party*", I signed up for updates only to try to understand the liberal perspective better. It hasn't helped at all.

In fact, from some of the posts I'm more confused about their train of thought than I was before. First off, I was hoping that this might be a group who could see that the current president was a tool of cronyism and entitlements spending. No such luck. In fact they can't even see that it exists. That doesn't really bother me though; it's an advantage they choose not to take. I do have to comment about the stupidest post though.

Apparently there was a political figure who made the statement that you should bring a knife with you, to protect yourself in a gunfight. The reason made for this is because you also get exercise because you have to get up close to the other person. Okay... How do you get more exercise when you're DEAD?

That's operating under the ridiculous notion that a lawbreaker will operate in a fair way. Really? What makes you think that a criminal, if not most people for that matter, won't take the action of self-interest? Their best interest is to take from you; yours is stopping that from happening. That's not just human nature that's a natural law! What makes anti-gun groups think law breakers will be stopped by more gun control? What is their incentive?

Another problem is a lack of evidence to support their claims. If gun control works so well, why do the states with the highest numbers of gun deaths have the strictest laws? Washington D.C., Detroit, Chicago, New York, all strict gun laws, all high murder rates.

Even the study by the *CDC* (this study was done to satisfy ObamaCare's gun law section. The CDC performing a study to tie gun control to healthcare? Nothing about this makes any sense what-so-ever!), the results of the study - 60% of gun deaths were suicides, after that deaths of criminals due to self-defense and dead last was deaths of innocent people by criminals. Even with the evidence being analyzed by a biased source, they still can't get the results to point their way. Another failed prohibition I would say.

Did we ever really need more than 15 Amendments?

Did we ever need more than 15 amendments? - No not really. I was rereading through my copy of the constitution, when I came to this conclusion - after a certain point the amendments have less to do with helping society as a whole and more to do with assisting certain demographics in society.

So, I'll start with the *15th* amendment "voting rights" no one has the right to vote - it's a privilege, but with this amendment an argument could be made that minorities have the "right" to vote. Same with the *nineteenth* ("women's voting rights") and section one of the *twenty-sixth* (eighteen years of age for the minimal age to vote), these are anti-discrimination laws, not voting rights laws.

Even worse than that is the *sixteenth* amendment "The congress shall have the power to lay and collect taxes on incomes… without apportionment among the several States without regard to any census or enumeration."

Reread that last part again "without apportionment among the several States without regard to any census or enumeration", basically unlike the other taxes "we the people" have to pay this one. This is a tax the government wanted so bad that it wasn't made simply into a law, but an amendment which is more difficult to get rid of. It needs to be repealed. Who does this amendment help, besides the feds that is?

Tax attorneys mostly, but everyone else not really. It's also the cause of our current convoluted and unfair tax system.

With the exceptions of the repeal of prohibition and the term limits for presidents, all the rest of the amendments since the early 1900's have caused more harm than good. They grant the government more power while catering to special interests and progressive causes. The only special interests the government should be catering to is in leaving the American citizens alone.

Law of the Land

The new retort by supporters of ObamaCare, during the push for defunding it is it's the "law of the land", so live with it. That's the most patronizing thing I've ever heard - and from the party that has made patronizing others an art form - that's impressive!

All this is yet another form of censorship of political speech by the Democratic Party, made by those who have legitimate exceptions to what they are doing. If they have the support of the populace on their side, why cower from this discussion? If they have the moral high ground, why not settle this?

Mostly it's because they know their constituencies understand just how deplorable these laws are, and would vote them out. They can't defend, not defunding, it's that simple.

When all you have is emotional rancor, it's hard to defend your point and that's all they've got. They voted "yes" to illegal laws and the "law of the land" seems to be take what you can, from whomever you can. The lawless have apparently taken over.

Guilty by Genetic Association

If you are white you have been ingrained with the perspective that we should feel that we have wronged all the different ethnic groups. The evidence, however, says something different from this though.

According to the Native Americans our ancestors forcibly drove them from their lands. The warriors of the tribes fought bravely to the end, but in the war parties, men, women and children of the white race were viciously murdered. Both sides had massive losses and killed innocent people. Should their modern descendants be held accountable for their actions?

The African Americans of this country were brought in as slaves by the Colonists. The slave trade was created by the other African tribes NOT by the white man. They would still be in Africa, engaged in civil war if not for the trade. Besides our founders were not comfortable with the practice and were looking to outlaw it from the get-go. Another point for consideration, what percentage of biological African heritage does someone need to have to claim racial sufferings. In other words at want point does your ancestry count you as "Black." There were a lot of rapes done by the slave masters, but escaped slaves attacked white women in retribution for their masters' actions. So many whites could have some black blood. Do the escaped slaves' descendants feel guilty for these acts of incivility?

The Mexican communities claim entitlement of land because the 'White Man,' chased them off it. Actually it was the Spanish and Native Americans that did the worst atrocities to the tribes of Latin America, than the Europeans. Many of the Mexican people alive today are from the conquistadors, not the Mexicana tribe which has the biological line has gone extinct. This land was BOUGHT from Mexico, not taken from them. Don't the Mexican people feel guilty for spreading this myth?

The Chinese were brought in for slave labor during the days of the railroads. They were the houseboys alongside the black slaves. They have had to suffer stereotypes as well as the other races. China has become one the most powerful countries in the world. Why don't they scream out for entitlements?

Social Activists want everything paid for by taxes, not caring that by using tax money, citizens might be supporting something that they find objectionable. How do they justify their anger?

Jews are a demographic that has been demonized and mistreated far worse than any other and they don't ask for any preferential treatment. Why don't they feel more entitled for the acts of atrocities by the descendants of Germany?

The American patriot who has to listen to all the contention, accusations and claims of entitlements. The one who should be the angriest. Where's his anger? He puts it aside because he loves his country and everyone else should follow his lead.

They are so Angry; They Get Angry when you Call Them Angry

I was reading a book by *New York Times,* columnist, Chris Hedges, *The Death of the Liberal Class* - well actually to be more precise I was *trying* to read it. It was so boring and angry - but most books by liberals and socialists are, and Chris Hedges is an admitted and devout socialist. But it was still good because it made me think, aside from the fact that I find socialism detestable and it's nothing more than pseudo-humanitarian drivel - it's also BORING!! That might be even more offensive than their social construction philosophies.

Even when I've disagreed with conservative or other libertarian authors, it's rare that I find them boring at least in their anger they make an insightful observation. Socialists don't do this, at least not when writing about literal policy ideas. When writing fictional stories, however, they are brilliant authors, such as H.G. Wells or George Orwell.

If nothing else with the imagery and the fantastic analogies, they draw the reader in and were entertaining. Hedges and other socialist authors who write about their cause in modern times have an appreciation for inspiration through anger, but they don't have appealing, satirical wit, of Orwell or the terrifying spectral imagery of Wells.

If Hedges wanted to gain a larger audience, even if they don't follow into his line of thinking, he should consider this. Then again there aren't a lot of socialist comedians out there - most probably got sent to the gulag for making fun of their glorious leader.

Animals are People too... Well, not Really

I'm an animal lover always have been, I've studied them as an adult as well as when I was a child. For over seven years I was working in a pet store. One of my favorite places to go in Las Vegas is Shark Reef. Performing acts of atrocities against animals is just plain wrong, but what is also wrong is the actions of animal rights groups to try and protect them. There are legal common sense actions that can be taken to protect the animals in a real way by getting public

129

support, but many of these groups don't care about public support and they should.

They frankly don't care who they hurt as long as the animals are saved - to hell with the people whose livelihood they ruin. I want to commend those who do things the right way first of all. Many victims of shark attacks have transformed into their most staunch defenders. This happened because after spending so much time trying to kill the beasts that took a part of their body away, they researched the animal and found out the ways in which the shark is persecuted by people.

Many species of shark (including the endangered ones) are being hunted for their fins, for shark fin soup. In Asia it's a delicacy, but many species are on the lists of either dinner or folk medicine, in that country. But this is nothing new, in America the first settlers of the West would kill the bison for its tongue, leaving the rest to rot. I have a problem with that, the needless waste; look at all that meat you're not using. Those in these shark rescue groups understand how important it is to have the public on their side and so they take every chance to educate the public about the problem and petition to have laws changed.

That is the right way to do this and these people treat the shark as what it is, an animal. The idiocy of those who don't act with regard to the public, base their arguments around one piece of flawed logic - animals have rights. Actually, no they don't. Rights are what a being of analytical thought, not survival instinct, possesses.

People are Animals too... Really!

It's amazing the people that are allowed, let alone encouraged to become tenured instructors in our most prestigious universities... Is it prestigious, or pretentious? Either way, we have Bill Ayers, the unrepentant bomber from the Weather Underground of the 1960's, who said, *"I feel we didn't do enough."*

Ward Churchhill, instructor of *Ethnics Studies* at the *University of Colorado*, made this statement about those who died in the *World Trade Center* on September 11, 2001, *"Well really, let's get a grip here shall we? True enough, they were civilians of a sort. But innocent? Gimme a break."* He goes further to say, *"If there was a better, more effective... way of visiting some penalty befitting their participation upon the little Eichmanns (Adolf Eichmann was the architect of the Holocaust for the Nazis) ... I'd be really interested in hearing about it."* Nowadays Bill Ayers lives with his memories of the *"good old days",* and Ward Churchhill is just one of many with an opinion and a big mouth. Comparatively, all their dangerous influence is felt by victims of their crimes from years ago and those in their classrooms, while it has scary potential, it is that - potentially, it might spur action of others. They are nothing compared to the next professor - Peter Singer.

Peter Singer teaches a course at Princeton University called, *Practical Ethics* and that's what he stipulates that ethics are practical, meaning more pragmatic and only to be adhered to when it suits

131

your needs. The self-appointed utilitarian philosopher will abandon morality if it clashes with his cause.

His main cause is that of animal rights, he has even been called the "godfather of animal rights", with the spark being struck with his 1975 book *Animal Liberation.* He took it to a very dark turn with another of his books *Defense of Animals,* in which he posed a provocative query - *Why do we experiment with* Chimps, *when the mentally handicapped are off limits? In this case they are the intellectually inferior.* The merits of the arguments may have some validity to them and the logical conclusion would be to consider halting animal testing on higher creatures. Problem solved, right? How is this dangerous, you might be wondering? It hinders research for diseases, but this story doesn't end here. See, Singer's logical conclusion wasn't only to stop animal testing, but instead to advance Eugenics in America.

Singer doesn't consider human life to be special and advocates euthanasia for the mentally and physically impaired. In the book *Practical Ethics,* he says, *"Killing a disabled infant is not morally equivalent to killing a person. Very often it is not wrong at all."*

Reason Magazine observes, *"Fetuses and some very impaired human beings are not persons in his view (*Singer's*) and have a lesser moral status than, say adult gorillas and chimpanzees."*

Singer has also stated numerously, that society should allow a "severely disabled" infant to be killed up to 28 days after the birth, at the parents' discretion - of course. When you have discussions about the most dangerous professors, in full scope of world impact, the Bill Ayers and Ward Churchhills come in second to advocates to infanticide. Where's that pseudo-humanitarianism now?

Clowning Around

There are a lot of times in the news I try to figure out how others in the media get to their opinions. How the Trayvon Martin case is more a showing an indication of racial tensions, than the backlash from it? How asking women to pay for their own contraceptives equates a war on women? Or how radical Islamic religions, that kill homosexuals and women are more tolerated, than Christian religions that - as a whole, simply find homosexuality and premarital sex to be wrong?

The most confounding story of all would have to be about the rodeo clown at a State Fair in Jefferson City, Missouri. A rodeo clown came out donning a mask of Barack Obama and what started as a joke at the expense of the president ended up as a twisted call of racial hatred. The Rodeo Association reprimanded the rodeo clown and banned him for life for this - a bit of an overreaction isn't it… but to the NAACP, that wasn't even enough. They wanted blood, they wanted a LAWSUIT! An overly sensitive observer (probably and Obama voter), who posted a picture of the event said it felt like being at a *Ku Klux*

Klan rally. A Klan rally, huh, because they have been to so many of those.

The Missouri House Democrats even hinted that taxpayer funding should be pulled from the event for this. This was a joke, nothing more. When did we get to the point that a joke could cause such a ruckus? How did a joke that caused no physical harm to anyone or property, lead to a possible lawsuit? Where are people's senses of humor? Oh I almost forget liberals don't have one.

There's Blood in the Water

I have always been fascinated by the subject of the law. I took a couple of Criminal Justice and Paralegal courses at the local college. In fact, the only reason I didn't go into law is because it requires so much schooling and I learn better on my own.

But what doesn't make sense is our criminal justice system; it doesn't really serve justice but the pockets of the agents of the law. Its flaw isn't in the design, but its execution. Lawyers are not encouraged to seek out the truth and protect the innocent, but rather fame and fortune. This has turned the system into a weight around the neck of American enterprise, turning it into drowning victims with hungry sharks swimming around it to take their pound of flesh.

So many great possibilities will remain, only possibilities because of this, essentially because of this litigious society we have here lost has its will to compete for fear of lawsuit. It's not worth the risk. To be fair the blame goes around, the lawyers who take these cases, also the media for creating the "quick payout" and "you're the victim" culture, the judges for not wanting to alienate anyone by throwing the absurd cases out, the general public for not saying anything about how stupid the cases are, and last of all the businesses themselves, for not having the guts to stand up for their companies. Okay maybe that's a little harsh, the business owners have some validity to their actions, the rest not so much.

From their point, those who go to court will usually lose and a settlement is cheaper financially, but the cost to the justice system and to the country itself has been far more detrimental. Somewhere along the line we have forgotten that the way to great products is through a series of inferior ones. It's called trial and error. That cup of coffee with an insecure lid was not negligence; it was a step in the road to a better one. The Mesothelioma that you or a loved one has was unintentional; it was from a lack of knowledge of the side effects of long term exposure to asbestos.

Another key part of the problem is people's feelings of entitlement and victimhood.

There was a very strange case (strange from start to finish) where a man bought a grill, only to find a man's chard leg in it. When the guy missing the appendage came to claim his leg, he wound up being sued by the man who bought the grill. The man claims since he bought the grill he was the rightful owner of the leg. This one had an ending with some sense and the man got his leg back, however, the other guy did get $5,000 for "compensation." But this is a relatively positive outlook in our country's legal system.

Remember the tobacco companies lawsuits. They might as well have marketed it this way, do you smoke? - sue the tobacco companies, they have money! Never mind that the package has a warning stating that you may develop health problems. Never mind that it jacks the price of the product up. Oh yeah, here's what you probably didn't know - the tobacco companies were in on the settlement. The racked in the money from it as well. Never mind all this because you got your part of this cash cow and got to stick it to the greedy capitalists (or so you thought at least) for something you did to yourself. Because to you, you're a victim and are due your "pain and suffering" settlement, but how much did you actually make in the scheme?

Nowhere near what your attorneys made. Neither what the tobacco companies made, but that's rarely the case. Many companies have had to shut down research and development on products, lay off their staff or shut down completely. This is why we don't have cures for many diseases, such as AIDS or cancer. The product risks don't outweigh the product benefits. It's no longer worth it to build a better mousetrap, not at the risk of breaking someone's finger who didn't read the directions or scaring them for seeing a dead mouse.

If You're Anti-War, Try Acting like It!

During the presidency of George W. Bush we heard rampant cries to end the wars in the Middle East, but now those cries have stopped. What happened? The wars didn't end; in fact we have added Libya and almost Syria. So where did the protesters go? Did they decide war isn't so bad? Funny how they disappeared when Bush did.

Rather than end the wars and close Gitmo, Obama has expanded both. He has turned on our allies and brought the countries that despise us into his circle, putting our foreign policy into the hands of America-haters. Yeah let's try that.

Even more than paying off those who hate our country, those in his cabinet who are supposedly opposed to war are now advocating it. Secretary of State, John Kerry made a statement saying that it was "immoral" for us not to intervene in Syria. Maybe so, but how is this any different from Vietnam? Kerry made his career out of continually saying it was immoral to intervene in Vietnam, even though their government was doing the same thing - so, why should the Syrian people be held in a higher regard than the Vietnamese?

That was even the same emotional rhetoric that Nixon's propaganda man used. Same as what Franklin Roosevelt said during World War II and Woodrow Wilson for World War I before him. The only real difference between the World Wars and the

137

rest, it was a reasonable conclusion that America would face an attack at some point, which would mean we would have a stake in the war, to defend ourselves.

That wasn't there with Vietnam, Korea or the Middle East. They are making sure a "State of Emergency" is maintained, because under it, the public is more compliant during a time of war. So from the perspective of those in power, perpetual war is a very promising prospect.

He Did it, Not Me

You ever meet someone and they make a special point of emphasizing how "honest" they are. "You can trust me," they might say. That's the way many politicians and law-makers operate, especially liberal ones.

Rather than sit back and wait to see the side effects of their bad law and do damage control, they claim the consequences of the law that were predicted, are from their opponents' interference against it.

The attacks on Paul Ryan after he presented his budget cuts to the Obama administration, when he claimed that the Affordable Care Act was not so "affordable" and it would gut Medicare, the democrats turned it on its head and claimed Ryan's proposed cuts were like "throwing grandma off the cliff." Oh hello again, emotional back mail, we missed you.

It was one more opportunity for a discussion of real world economics in politics shoved off the side of a cliff. This happens all the time and mostly because when it comes to information the general public is lazy. They take the first report they get as truth, instead of questioning everything.

Prior to the information age, there was very little choice, thanks to the "Fairness Doctrine" all information was filtered through the FCC but now there's no excuse. There's probably millions of bloggers and independent news sites to choose from, so if you want your information without all the emotional manipulation - you can have it your way.

The Return of the Twinkie

Whenever people talk about how great unions are and that they help the little guy, I have one word for them - Twinkies. What happened to the Hostess Company was an atrocious act of bullying by the unions and one of the most extreme cases of pseudo-humanitarianism for the "workers," since the Industrial Revolution. It shows just how little unions care about the little guys and only about getting their dues from their members, if they did care about their little guys they would have old them to stop before the situation got that far.

139

Part of the problem is the union leaders encourage the mindset the company belongs to the employees and that they actually own the jobs - that their position is "theirs" as well. It really belongs to the employer; the company, the jobs and the benefits, all to offer to whomever is the most qualified. That's how it should be too!

The employer is the one who took the calculated risks of setting up a company, taking the chance of failure. The employer did the research and development - or paid a specialist to do it -to test the market for his or her company. The employer is the one who sacrificed time and money to develop a company, the reason you have a job to begin with.

That's what the union leaders have curiously left out. They also don't consider how *little* sacrifice the union members have made for "their" company. In the high market companies, they get benefits, at times very amazing ones at that and all for doing their jobs. That's where the employees are really cleaning up! Even the bad employees get these perks as long as they stay with the company for so long a time. But bad employees don't get other perks - maybe your work performance or lack of experience, is the reason you didn't get that raise or promotion. To unions that doesn't matter though.

Unions are not the voice of the little guy, but they are his roadblock to success. Unions don't think practical economics works, but it looks like their union members don't either.

Charity's Good but a Job Would be Better

The arguments from the left are amusing to say the least, especially when it comes to entitlements spending as not only a necessary evil but as a beneficial tool for the masses - it goes from the extremes of emotional propaganda to religious sentiments (doesn't that violate the separation of *Church and State*? Apparently not if you're liberal).

In a statement by Charlie Rangel, if you vote down entitlements spending "you would be going to hell." Responsible spending is going to send me to hell? That's what the real question here is - with all the insanity of the way taxpayer money is spent by these drunken sailors, I think God will forgive me if I don't give them another penny.

Whatever charity I do give to are local ones, so that if there's a possible impropriety - it's easier to follow up on. That's the best argument for doing business locally, you can see where your money is being spent and those who are not acting in the right can be addressed. When they are miles away or across the country, that's a different matter.

But for the record "charity" and "social programs" are two completely different concepts - Charity is completely voluntary, you give what you can, when you can, to those whose cause you support; Social Programs on the other hand are forced (give or get penalized, with the charge of Tax Evasion), that

141

you have to give when you're told, to whomever the government decides for you. See the problem?

Under social programs anyone who fits inside their rigid guidelines gets money. Illegal immigrants, they get money; oppressed minorities, they get money; unions, they get a *lot* of money; as do special interests and lobbyists.

The biggest problem with social programs - they don't help anyone, not really. The areas where the poverty and the crime rates are the highest, are also where the government spending in social programs are the highest as well, and this is every ethnic group. Blacks, Hispanics, Asians, Whites and Native Americans, all live in squalor in areas of government housing.

When you look at life on Indian reservations over the areas where they have to make it on their own - the differences are astounding. In the government reservations, its ramshackle shanties that look like that of a third world country, rampant poverty; but the ones who are responsible for themselves, live in mansions. You can look around and see that with every group, those who had to work for it live better. As good as the intentions may have been, it appears the drive to succeed is more rewarding than a promised payment without the work.

Capitalists Genocide

Turn on the news and wait a couple of minutes, you will be bombarded with comments from the leaders of the nation condemning the "evil" and "despicable" capitalists. How they all are callous, cold, uncaring and solely responsible for the woes of the general public or at the very least keeping the poor, poor. But a little secret that the anti-capitalists won't tell you - they are in fact ardent capitalists themselves, but even worse they are also monopolists.

Let's start with Nancy Pelosi and her involvement with Lion's Gate Limited and the building of the Cordevalle Golf Course and Resort in San Martin, CA. In 1996, the Santa Clara County Planning Commission reluctantly granted a small group of investors a permit with restrictions to keep it a mostly public usage course and abide by environmental concerns, that were designed to protect a couple of endangered species in the area of the site.

Both restrictions were ignored, with the club rules including that nonmembers pay $275.00 for 18 holes and give seventy-two hours' notice before tee-time. Even when these excessive conditions were met the common reply to the public trying to play was, "Sorry, we're full" so much for "public" access, as well as showing Pelosi's blatant hypocrisy in environmental matters and her claim to be helping the "little guy", it also demonstrates her willingness to capitalize at the expense of others.

How is Pelosi not a heartless capitalist? How about the Clintons? They are "middle class" folks and not about the money. Then why did they use their friends' to petition luxury retailers for more than $190,000 in gifts before leaving the White House near the end of Bill's last term, and another $360,000 donated to the White House. All of which ended up being used in the Clinton's home remodel in Chappaqua.

While the Clintons have claimed to others to pay more in taxes, they pay 7% less than others in their tax bracket claiming hundreds of thousands in write-offs. Another disappointment for those true anti-capitalists.

At least they got Ralph Nader - surely Nader, the man that has made it his life's mission to protect us from corporate greed isn't a capitalist himself - surely, he is. While he claims to live the modest life in a small apartment in Washington DC, his true residence is a $2 million home in Bancroft Place. It's not in his name though but that of one of his siblings. Maxine Cheshire of the *Washington Post*, had this to say after asking Nader about the house, " he's [Nader] so excited about the whole idea of tax write-offs and all that... that's the greatest investment you can make (owning your own home), the biggest tax advantage."

Nader also commands the best of things when traveling during a speaking engagement, a representative of the trial lawyer association told *Forbes* magazine "limousines and nothing but the best hotels." So much for the icon of frugality, sounds more like a rockstar on tour.

What about Noam Chomsky, professor, socialist and self-appointed "champion of the ordinary guy" a socialist wouldn't use the capitalist system, would he? Think again, to keep up the illusion of his socialist philosophies he dresses drab and keeps a low-key manner, but don't be fooled. While Chomsky goes around fighting against the militarization of America in public, in private he's been profiting off it - being paid by the Research Laboratory of Electronics a group funded by the Pentagon. Due to his standing in academia he has not been properly vetted for this clear hypocrisy. If you can't trust a socialist, who can you trust?

We end with the "documentary" filmmaker Michael Moore, made famous by his condemnation of America and its capitalist structure. Moore is even eager to attack his fellow liberals, for their extravagant lifestyles. The young Moore is hardly the victim of capitalism - his father owned his home, had a couple of cars, he and his siblings went to private schools and were able to go to college.

Moore has never known the poverty he claims, in one Canadian newspaper he stated he has always lived under $12,000 a year - apparently he forgot about that $50,000 advance from a New York publisher for a book about General Motors, or the article in *Mother Jones* for another $50,000, or a grant for $20,000 from Ralph Nader.

The "titan of the working man", doesn't live in Flint, Michigan anymore either, but a ten acre lot by Torch Lake, considered one of the most beautiful lakes in the world by *National Geographic*. The small family run business Blue Chips Log Homes would more than likely contest the claim of Moore being a friend to the "little guy", since they had to put a lien on his house to get the dead-beat millionaire to pay up. Moore also flies on a private jet and is accompanied by a convoy of SUVs with armed

145

bodyguards.

For people so ardently against capitalism, this den of thieves sure seems to enjoy the perks of the system and to keep others out of it.

Chapter **EIGHT**

EMBRACING THE "WHITE" STATES: THE TWO PARTY CONUNDRUM

In my studies of popular culture I have learned that the conventional wisdom, when it pertains to the independent parties, the duopoly holds the country hostage. But in my analysis I have found very little evidence to support their claim of superiority. That's where the "white" states come in. The "white" states in this case, have nothing to do with race, rest assured, but it has to do with what white represents.

On a monochromatic color wheel, white is the point in which all colors combine. It's a very fitting analogy since most independent parties are a combination of the policies of the two major parties.

3 Million Voters can be Wrong

Before **going into the topic**, I want to get the record straight on what I am referring to with the terminology "white states," this has nothing to do with race, on the visible light spectrum white is the point where all colors converge. Many of the policy ideas in the third parties are similar to the republican and democrats, but the philosophies are different, but that's what I was referring to.

Libertarian and Constitutionalist party philosophies are varying mixes of social liberties with responsible economic policy. Socialism has similar social programs as the Democrats, but understands the importance of minimal regulations. Now onto the topic of this segment.

In the 2012 election the Democrats have been claiming an amazing total victory over the Republicans. The Obama victory was monumental in their eyes and showed that so many wanted him to stay in office. That's not the whole story though.

Let's look at the numbers: Obama won reelection by 3 ½ million votes, that's not a huge victory really and will shrink even more when you bring in all the factors.

Three million republican voters chose not to go to the voting booths, because they couldn't vote for Romney. This was thanks to the colluded efforts by those running against Romney for the GOP nomination, especially, Newt Gingrich, Rick

Santorum and Michelle Bachmann. Some claim Ron Paul also had a part in it, but his supporters wouldn't have voted republican anyway, they more than likely voted for Gary Johnson or wrote in Ron Paul.

To be fair to Gingrich and Santorum they did (eventually) give Romney their blessing and support - even though it was less than sincere on Santorum's part - Bachmann never did. But their time quibbling against each did have a lasting effect.

Combine that with the voters who couldn't vote for a Mormon, Obama's "stellar" handling of Hurricane Sandy, Chris Christie's being overly cordial to Obama, Romney's comments were being blown out of proportion and his not being aggressive enough during the final two debates, well that's how we wound up with four more years.

In all this my major problem is that these people didn't even consider voting for one of the third party candidates. If they had issues with Romney and would *never* vote Obama, that's fine try looking at one of the other parties. Check out the libertarians, constitutionalists or unaffiliated parties. Give both the two major parties a reason to be nervous with that statement. In the process you might learn maybe you have more in common with the other parties, than the "lesser of two evils."

They Bought What!

Who thinks the government spends your tax dollars responsibly? If you said no, then good, you pay attention at least to a degree. If you said yes, you're in for a shock. Do you think $25,000 to $45,000 for a portrait of each of the presidents is responsible?... You paid for that. How about the remodeling costs of the White House and Oval Office? Or the thousands that G.W. Bush spent remodeling the bathroom?

You can't take tours of "the people's house", but at least they get to live like royalty. So what if you have to work three jobs to make ends meet, as long as the White house gets new tile! But this is only the beginning, there's a lot more things that the government has wasted money on, like:

* $200 million a year is spent to advertise associations and co-op products in foreign markets. One is a reality show in India shown advertising U.S. cotton- brought you by the Department of Agriculture.*

*   *The EPA awarded a $141,450 grant under the Clean Air Act to fund a Chinese study for the U.N. to promote clean fuel.*

*   *Amtrak, has stayed federally funded despite the fact it is losing money because of food service expenses. In 2011, its loss was $84.5 million and has a ten year total loss of $833.8 million.*

*   *The U.S. Navy bought 450,000 gallons of bio fuels for $12 million, equal to $27 per gallon, in an effort to help commercialize bio fuels.*

A grant of $325,000 was given to the National Science Foundation to create a "RoboSquirrel" a realistic-looking animatron to study how a rattlesnake would react to it... Good to see they are not wasting money!

$2 million was given to the cupcake industry in Small business loan guarantees.

Improper SNAP payments account for $2.8 billion in abuse.

A Community Development Block Grant in the amount of $750,970 went to the Smuttynose Brewery, despite their financial success.

$520,000 went to fix the Stevenson Road Covered Bridge in Green County, Ohio. The bridge has not been used in ten years.

A super conductor originally allotted for $5 billion went up to $12 billion, before it was scrapped- at only partially built. It was "used to store Styrofoam cups" until purchased by private interests at "pennies on the dollar."

In 2003, $25 billion in government spending went unaccounted for.

A school district purchased a pizza machine for $725,000; it was expected to "churn out 800 pizzas a day to sell to other various campuses in the district." Due to frequent mechanical errors it made only 2,000

150

pizzas in 2 years.

*In Indiana, a Limestone Pyramid was planned to increase tourism with a total of $700,000 spent. The abandoned site is "little more than a giant rock pile."

*The Teton Dam in Idaho, cost $100 million, cracks in the dam appeared which broke causing an addition $2 billion worth of damage.

*Medicare spending in 2008 included, "billions in questionable claims" for diabetic shoes for amputees, wheelchairs for sprained wrists and walkers for confirmed paraplegics.

*The Cross-Florida Bridge Canal, planned as a bridge to connect the Atlantic Ocean with the Gulf of Mexico, sold as a job creator during the Great Depression, to end up "a $120 million partial scar across the state.

*Railhead- an online terrorist database was infested with mismanagement and government abuse. "Potentially hundreds of millions of dollars have been wasted", because of a better system the project was scrapped and the $500 million earmarked went to renovating one of the Boeings buildings.

*A highway tunnel in Boston nicknamed, "Big Dig" was originally estimated to cost $2.5 billion ballooned to $22 billion, not to be paid off fully until 2038.

36,000 Department of Defense were involved in a credit card scam. $623 million in official travel expenses were charged to government credit cards.

In 2004, in another travel expenses error $100 million was spent by the DOD on airline tickets that were never used or refunded. The Pentagon reimbursed at least $8 million to employees who never used the tickets. Meanwhile, the rest of us get zero!

Get your Hands off my Legislature you Damned, Dirty Libertarians

This past year the Libertarian party has been getting a lot more attention than ever before, especially by the Republican Party. What's the reason for this? Well, it's mostly because the general public are getting tired of this duopoly system that our political system is has failed them and this is causing them to consider the other options. Basically, the fringe party of the libertarian is looking more appealing all the time. In fact, in polls 60% of the public say they would consider voting for a third party candidate.

Its actions are matching its words for one thing and its representatives are consistent with a clear message. Freedom and choice, it's that simple.

The two major parties don't think these things are important.

The Republican Party - supposedly the party of small government and freedom - has shown an odd attitude of contempt, to this surge of libertarianism. Mostly it has been from establishment republicans like, John McCain and Lindsey Graham. Take the infamous Rand Paul filibuster, McCain's response was to call him a, "wacko bird," quite the comprehensive analysis senator! Keep in mind that's how he feels about the Libertarian Party and those who think protecting civil rights are important; they are not in their right minds to him. That's sad since its part of his job to protect the rights of the people. I think he's forgotten about the fourth amendment and he would feel differently if those drones he's so comfortable with were buzzing around his home. How about his office in Washington... No, don't like that? Didn't think so. But it's okay for the people to give up their rights, I see.

Senator Lindsey Graham's conduct hasn't been any better or less questionable! His response to the filibuster was to back up McCain and he added, "President Bush used drones... I applaud him (President Obama) for using such tactics."

Senator Orrin Hatch of Utah had to get in the game too, after he won back his chair form opponent Dan Lilenquist - Lilenquist was favored among libertarians. After winning Hatch came out condemning the Libertarian party, the only plus with McCain and Hatch is this is supposed to be their last terms as senators. South Carolina, pleases do us all a favor and make it Graham's last one too!

Not that all those scoring points with this anti-libertarian mindset are veteran politicians, bring in New Jersey Governor, Chris Christie. This quasi-libertarian movement in the GOP made him very uncomfortable in his statement he actually referred to it as *"a dangerous idea."* Dangerous, Governor? More dangerous than a bloated overreaching government? More dangerous than senators and congressmen who have forgotten their place?

That's the bad news but there's good news too, many in the Republican (and the Democrats as well) are willing to work with libertarians and have even praised their efforts of constitutional purity and economic responsibility.

Rand Paul has already been mentioned and has been seen with the Libertarian icons, like Glenn Beck and Judge Andrew Napolitano. Others with similar views are Ted Cruz, Mike Lee and Justin Amash. Jim DeMint and Sarah Palin both have praised the Libertarian party. DeMint even met with *Reason TV* for an interview by their founders, saying that Ron Paul is right in his economic policies and the republicans should listen. Palin is a far craftier and brighter woman than given credit and her actions her are proof of that. She sees the change in demographic and instead of fighting it - she is embracing it.

Democrats will work with libertarians on as well, Ron Paul has worked with their members like Denis Kucinich on social issues. This is the way to have a working government, work together on policies of agreement and don't be afraid to hurt their feelings on issues of disagreement. We don't have to agree with everyone, every time; we have to be true to ourselves.

Republican Rehab

Before the 2008 elections I considered myself a republican but once they got John McCain as the nominee I started exploring the other options.

Now I knew I wasn't a democrat, because I knew setting up financial policy using your heart and not your head would lead to trouble. But I also saw how full of it democrats are, many of the policies that were supposed to help others didn't do so - they helped those who came up with the laws. So, I kept looking. I checked out the Green party, no I'm not a hard-core environmentalist, but a practical one adopting only the concepts that were practical. Not a socialist either, I feel too strongly about my property rights and despise unions.

In the end it was the Libertarian party that I found myself agreeing with more than any, it lets others make their own choices on social issues but the taxpayer doesn't pay for it. If you agree, maybe you're a Libertarian, too. I came up with a little test that, I will present for you know:

The Independent Thought Quiz

1) War should be used

a) To frighten others into submission
b) As a tool to meet an end
c) With restraint and infrequently, it could be used to get the citizens to give up their rights

2) Morality should be:

a) Controlled by the government
b) Decided by special interests
c) Be up to the people to decide and live with the consequences

3) The Constitution is:

a) Flexible
b) Antiquated
c) To be strictly adhered to

4) More choices are:

a) Too confusing
b) Unnecessary let the government decide
c) Great, more choices means everyone can find what they need

5) The third parties:

a) Are scary
b) Are stupid, even two is too many
c) What the country needs

Alright, pencils down let's so how you did. If you picked all A's, you have more in common with the Republicans. If you picked all B's you're a Democrat. Either way you should keep reading.

If you picked C's, then you have more in common with the Libertarian or Constitutionalist parties - Welcome aboard, you Wacko Bird!

Democrat Denial

Have you ever tried to talk politics with a democrat? It's not much fun. They're stubborn and can't ever conceive of a minute possibility they are wrong.

As bad as it can be sometimes to debate a member of the GOP, at least most of them are eager to engage in an actual discussion and defend their point. Democrats as a whole want to shut you up and close off the discussion as quickly as they can.

If you disagree with them you must be wrong and silenced, because we can't have any contrary perspectives out there. Oh no, that can't be tolerated!

Their opinion is the only the one that is valid and the rest must be eliminated in any way possible, remember they are doing it for the "greater good" so whatever they do is justified in the end. We mustn't forget that they went to *Harvard*, so they know everything. They know what is right for you (despite the fact they have never even met you). They know how to do your job better than you (even though they don't know what you do for a living, and probably haven't even read anything on it). They know what you should think and believe (never mind they haven't had your experiences and don't know what you have learned).

If any of the conclusions you've made match the ones in the italics, then you might want to start paying attention because the choices are being made *for* you. If you disagree with them speak up now, while you are still allowed to speak.

The Worst Laws ever Written

We hear all the time that the parties need to come together, Republicans need to give in and we have to make sure we get the laws passed. It doesn't matter if it hurts the general public; it takes away our rights or comprising their principles or those of the parties, but it has to be passed to know what's in it.

Well, the best way to show the logic fallacy in all this, is to present the laws passed under the flag of "partisianship" that have made our lives worse:

The McCain Feingold Act- Later renamed the Bipartisian Campaign Reform Act; *this bill turned into law, doesn't fix the problem of corporate money influence in presidential elections – but instead, creates a form of censorship that political ad, paid for by corporations, can't be shown 30 to 60 days before* an election. Supposedly, with its legal limits of the amount of money that can be contributed by corporations, it has claimed to take that power and give it back to the American people; but determined powerful individuals got around that by giving money to multiple corporations and funneling it to their candidate.

Chemical Safety Improvement Act- All disclaimers and notices on chemicals don't make life any safer, and increase the costs for businesses. There is a lot of room for abuse in this law.

Firearm Owner Protection Act- This law turned back the tide of illegal gun restrictions of the Gun Control Act of 1968; however, it also banned the sale of machine guns - after the date of the bills' implementation - to civilians and restricted it to Military and Law Enforcement. Political Scientist, Earl Kruschke commented "approximately 175,000 automatic firearms have been licensed....and evidence suggests that none of these weapons has ever been used in a violent crime,' Aside from the machine gun ban, this actually a beneficial bill.

Protecting Lawful Transport of Firearms Act- This is a law that actually protects gun owners, but the infringement by a few state governments – notably, New York and New Jersey – has been misinterpreting their power in regards to this bill ever since the enactment of the Firearm Owner Protection Act.

Trade Promotion Act- This act put the power of

trade issues in the hands of the executive branch and limits the congress' power in trade to a vote of yes or no, without power to make revisions.

*Immigration Law Revision- The Immigration law, by the "gang of eight" doesn't fix the problems in Immigration, making it easier for legal immigrants or cutting incentives for illegal immigrants. It keeps all the flaws in our immigration policies.

So, do you still think partisan politics are a bad thing?

Letting Go

Those who are part of the duopoly don't realize how hard it is to change from one of the two parties, to one of the "fringe" parties. But if you don't think you are really a republican or a democrat it's worth it to find out more about the other options and make the change.

You will feel alone at times, but you're not - not at all. That feeling of being alone is what the duopoly creates and capitalizes on, that's how they maintain control, making people feel they are "throwing your vote away." Minimize all legitimate party options and go head to head with the "opposition", but this opposition is not a real opposition at all - they agree far too much.

In a poll by the *Cato Institute* their results was

that the 8% of the people who are libertarian in philosophies is a myth… it's a far higher percentage! When polled on values and philosophies 21% is the real number of potential libertarian voters and it's continuing to grow. There are many who feel having more choices than two parties are a better option.

When the democratic party was created, the voters didn't have a choice - it was one faction of the republican party versus another (where does that sound familiar).This lack of choices in voting is what we have again and like in the past the cure is to bring more choices. Changing our finance laws is the first step to bring more choices. Many even institute the alternate or popular vote, where instead of a coin toss it's a ranking voting system. Or many somebody will, or has, come up with another way to fix the system. If more of us realize that more choices work best than we can return this country to its former glory.

Politicians Behaving Badly

A general consensus is that politicians in modern times are getting a free pass for unethical behavior that they wouldn't have before. There might be legitimacy to that claim, but an act of leniency on the part of the general public isn't the full story.

Newt Gingrich's tryst took place during the Clinton White House, same with Dick Morris. The example of disregard for the respect for taxpayer money by the Obama administration has led to the CIA, GSA, and scandals by other government organizations. Just as the moral scandals were due to the examples set by the previous administrations leads.

This is not to validate the actions of ethical or financial slip-ups by, Newt, Dick or these government entities, but to remind the presidents that their actions set the tone for the way the country is going to be run. For a few of the presidents - it sounds like they hit the "Brown Note."

Real Change

The only way to be an effective political campaign is to spend massive amounts of money, starting in the millions of dollars, right?

Well, maybe not, if you can come up with an appealing and eye catching ad and create a buzz about it on social media, it is possible to compete without spending a lot.

Take the Herman Cane campaign - he didn't have the money of Romney or Obama - so his team thought outside the box and he was leading in the polls. If not for a scandal he might have been the contender against Obama! His brilliant team used small budget ads - one being made for a staggering $380.00. They dared to be different and it paid off big.

He showed fiscal restraint, but this kind of

success is unfortunately rare. More times than not it doesn't work out this way, but it begs the question - is that lack of success because of a failure to connect or a failure to collect?

It's true that one of the factors in Obama's favor was money, but he also utilized social media. McCain and Romney did not. Could that be the real key to success, now and in the future? It's worth investing in that's for sure.

Constitution Needs Review not Rewriting

"He fucking hates Ted Cruz. He hates his style…" Was that the comments from a democrat, Harry Reid maybe, Dick Durbin, or Charlie Rangel?

Actually it wasn't from any democrat - but a member of the Republican Party; it was a spokesman for none other than John McCain. So, what about Ted Cruz's "style" does the senator despise? Does that mean he hates what the GOP is supposed to stand for - constitutional practices such as, privacy rights, the right to self-preservation, property rights, or the right to free market decisions vs. entitlement policies? Does that mean he approves of ObamaCare?

Ted Cruz was the one in the right here, he was standing up (in every way) to the dictatorial over-reach of Obama and his minions. Isn't that part of the job of a representative of the people, to defend their rights? Or to keep the promises made to their constituency?

Some of the senators have said they can't stand with Cruz - because they feel he doesn't go far enough! I can respect that, is that the reason of senator McCain, or does he simply not want to rock the boat (again)? Is that the reason with Lindsey Graham as well? They don't want to put their necks on the line; despite that what the people of their states have said they wanted? This descent from constitutionality is nothing new for McCain or Graham, or other members of the senate or congress, but for how much longer are "we the people" going to let them do it? I for one say, no more.

Maybe Partisanship does Work

A lot of people say that partisan politics are dividing the nation and we have to come together to fix the problems, but the observation I've made is this is not the case at all. It's good that we have different and distinct ideas and philosophies, its good we have discourse and open debate. The different suggestions mean we are all engaged and everyone's perspective is being considered.

I want to hear and understand what others think and how they come to their conclusions. I want to understand why federalists think expanding the government is good or why this option is more valid than any others. The problem isn't the diverse opinions, but a lack of respect for those contrary opinions. Partisanship itself is a good thing - it protects us from the earlier laundry list of bad laws. If the McCain Feingold Act had been properly debated the unintended consequences may have been noticed and this stupid law might have died out.

Chapter **NINE**

DOGMATIC TYRANNY

People do some very strange, if not downright stupid things in the name of God. The chapter is about the worse actions committed because of theological beliefs.

Lost their Heads

Every **religion has its** extremist sects to them; atheism, paganism, Muslim, Christianity, and Judaism, all have their fringe groups interpreting their religious texts for the purpose of hate. Most of them have already seen their religions call to violence come and go - the radical Muslims are still in the period of violence.

Many peaceful members of the Muslim religion say that the Koran, their version of the bible, does not espouse such acts of violence against others. Detractors say they are lying, I don't know since I've never read it, but I will say this - reading an extreme view of religious teachings is nothing new. Whether it's beheadings by radical Muslims, the hangings by the Christian White Supremacists, beating at the word of Jesses Jackson by racial ideologues or the vitriol shouted out by the Westboro church, all are in the wrong.

Religion is supposed to be about love, isn't it? The teachings of God are supposed to give peace and how to respect others and their opinions isn't it? Theology is about making us better human beings not become more like the beast, correct? But the actions of these breeders of religious hatred are embracing the beast; they are acting on the tribal man instincts that lie dormant.

Why do they do it? If they are so full of hate, why not walk away from religion - rather than fixate on it? Because they have convinced themselves that they are the right - this is their cause and they cannot stop! In their minds, their interpretation of God and his law will smite them if they stop their quest. The surprise for them will be when they meet their maker and have to answer for their hatred. Oh won't that be fun!

Night of Evil, or Escape from Convention

October 2012 - On the *Five* on *Fox News*, Bob Beckel made one of the most asinine comments ever; he intimated that we should no longer celebrate Halloween - because it is a celebration of evil and a pagan holiday. Both these assertions are wrong, but based on quasi-truth.

First, off Halloween is a day to honor the dead, not a celebration of evil. What his conclusion is based on is the culture's modern customs associated with the holiday, but these customs are important since they are a much needed deviation from the norm. It's an *artificial* evil not a *genuine* evil.

Second, the holiday itself is not a pagan holiday, but celebrated during the same day as one. The original name is a tip off of its real ties - "All Saint's Day", does that sound pagan to you? The confusion here is because, not only when it's celebrated, but also many of its traditions are the same as the pagan holiday. *Samhain,* from the pagan religion, Halloween is confused for is the celebration of the fall harvest and a time when the dead could revisit the earth and the first Christians decided their holiday should be on the same day as this.

But the early Christians did this on purpose to try to minimize the pagan religions and destroy the pagans. Most of the customs in our Christian holidays have pagan origins - The Jack O' Lantern, the Christmas Tree, the Easter Egg, just to name a few.

Some of our traditions have unusual ties, but what they contribute to society is important. There are members of the public that would like to destroy such customs because they are uncomfortable with them, but that is not for them to decide. We need these deviations from the norms and maybe if we aren't so determined to be offended by them and jump to conclusions based on false information - we can enjoy them. At the very least we should not spoil other people's fun, as long as it's not physically harming others or their property. So to Mr. Beckel, I would say - Loosen up!

Whatever Happened to Santa Claus?

Why does the idea of children believing in Santa Claus, the Tooth Fairy or the Easter bunny, bother some people so much? It doesn't make sense, shouldn't we be encouraging children to use their imaginations and live in a fantasy world?

It helps them as adults to be creative, if they are accustomed to dreaming big as children they will dream big as adults. Why would we want to take them from them?

Putting that aside for a moment, what's so wrong with Santa Claus as being a model for the principles and virtues he represents? He was charitable, honest and loving; shouldn't we be trying to encourage children to believe in him as long as they can?

Even some Christians argue against the Claus saying he's one more distraction against the true meaning of the holiday- distraction from the true meaning of Christmas? A man who, in his life, did anonymous charitable work for children. He's not a distraction, he's a perfect embodiment of the holiday - he's the embodiment of impartial, pure, unadulterated love.

How can having Santa Claus associated with the holiday of loving your fellow man be a bad thing? This is another case of theological anger. It's not enough that Santa Claus died, now those he served have to kill him as well.

"God hates Fags"

"God hates Fags"... **Stop** for a minute and let that really sink in. Now that is the mantra of a church, the recently infamous - Westboro Church. If you look it

up, the name of their webpage is *"God hates Fags!"*

This is a radical sect of the Baptist church movement and should be noted that the other Baptists churches have gone on record that Westboro doesn't reflect their views and find what they are doing to be very extreme and distasteful.

For the record I think I would consider their rhetoric to be borderline blasphemous, the real problem with their motto is the "God hates" in it. Whoever or whatever God is, he doesn't hate anyone. We all are his children are we not? That's what I'm always told anyway, and that God loves all, doesn't he? So is there any truth in the phrase *"God hates Fags?"* Of course not, he might not approve of the lifestyle but hate them, no.

Christians should pay attention to these theological zealots though, because they will be ones non-Christians will associate with Christianity. Yes, with some it will happen anyway, but you can do damage control and proactively go on record saying their views are extreme.

Their views are not the views of God, but one of anger and hate, who does that sound more like? It's not man's moral authority to judge others after all, right? Christ could have joined in stoning the prostitute, but instead he embraced her - he treated her like a person, and like the rest of us she was flawed. Are you so perfect, don't you have flaws? Guess what, if you're judging others their personal choices, than you are flawed.

So, do you think you have the right to cast the first stone - like the members of the Westboro Church - or would you rather help your fellow man, as the one in whose name you claim to act would?

Scientology: What were we thinking?

What is scientology exactly? Seriously, I want to know, what is it? It's not a religion, I'm told - but it's categorized as a church, does that make it a philosophy? Or is it even simpler than that and one more entry in the list of cults?

That's what it is, a cult - they have emotional manipulation, tell you to abandon your friends and family, fleece you for as much money as they can and isolate you from society in a large compound. Sounds like a cult to me! If you've studied cults these are the same tactics that cult leaders use too. It's to make you feel as vulnerable as possible, so you will submit. The scientology movement does have one major flaw that makes it easier to dismiss, tha most cults - it's founder's history. As much as the members would want to ignore that L. Ron Hubbard is the greatest liability to the movement.

What is it about Hubbard that makes him an easy target for his detractors? He's a science fiction writer and the basic premise of scientology sounds like it came from a 1960's B-movie. Coming to a city near you, it's - *Invasion of the Soul Snatchers* rated S - for you have serious self-esteem issues if you fall for this shit!

This is how cults operate, find those who are outsiders and enlist them into their ranks. Better yet appeal to the charismatic (and in the case of scientology, the *Hollywood* elite) and the "rebels." That's what I find so amusing in all this; these supposed "rebels" being treated like frat house pledges to join an organizational hierarchy. *Yes sir, may I have another!*

The lost will give up their idealism in the struggle to find themselves, when an individual with a strong message and a gait of authority comes along. It happened with Jim Jones and L. Ron Hubbard, it will continue to if those who blindly follow refuse to wake up… don't give up your analytical thought in the spur of the moment if it doesn't feel right. If that little voice in your head says take your family and run - do it! You deserve better than the L. Ron Hubbards of the world.

Will the Meek Inherit the Earth

Humility has never been one of my virtues, mostly because I feel it's an over-rated one. This might strike you as a disingenuous claim on my part, if I'm not humble than why do I remind readers that my writings are conjecture and not hard-hitting facts? Honesty mostly, but also because I want others to be as open with my opinions as I am with theirs. It's a basic respect thing, but humility has nothing to do with it.

The problem with humility in the real world is most others see it as something of little value and will minimize it before you can get them to hear you out. If you're humble you're underestimated, that is something you can capitalize on, that's capitalize, not take advantage of. You can capitalize without being a bully.

As I say "why make an enemy on a point of contention, when we can make an ally on a mutual consent." It's far more advantageous to all involved.

Another reason you should be more open to contrary opinions, is because you might wind up learning something. At times it's about the issues, sometimes science, or human nature, or even about yourself. Learning to see the world through their eyes, understanding our differences, is the only way to really make a difference in this world.

Whether making an ally or sharpening your argument civility pays, this kind of thinking may sound paradoxical to my original point, but that's where the faulty logic is proven in and of itself.

The meek in the end may inherit the earth, but it's the diligent and strong-willed that will alter it - for better or worse.

"So help me God"

Recently a debate has ensued about whether or not to take down a poster at the Air Force Academy because it has the oath that the cadets take, which contains the phrase *"So help me God"* in it, but removing the poster is only the beginning of the debate - because now the Religious Freedom Foundation wants to remove the phrase from the oath altogether. Well, why not compromise on this and let the "offensive" phrase be voluntary, that was one of the suggestions and it was shot down.

Nothing short of eliminating the phrase and taking down the poster will do. The group's spokesman, Mikey Weinstein, also stated the poster misquoted the oath anyways, so why not take it down for that instead of attacking others freedom of religious speech?

As for it's supposed "violation" of the establishment clause, let's be crystal clear with the wording and its original inference - terms like, *"so help me God"* or *"under God"* are going by a utilitarian definition of God and not a specific God, just as silent prayer or a moment of silence, are universal to most religions. If this poster was mentioning God as interpreted by one religion that would be one thing, but even their claim for this reason is invalid. Pretty much every religion believes in God in some form, so there's really no logic to their argument and only an agitator would have the desire to pursue this.

Another argument in favor of this action, in this particular case was that President John Quincy Adams was sworn to office on a stack of law books rather than the bible - that's right; he *voluntarily* opted out of taking the oath on the bible, like the original suggestion for those objecting to the phrase could opt out of as well.

Finally, in the claim that having this poster is a violation of the constitution - I think those people need to reread it. To take the poster down, would be the violation to the constitution and Freedom of Speech. Proponents of these courses of actions, violate the rights of those who do believe in God (not only Christians) and the rights of those who put up the poster. Those who are offended by it don't have to recite the oath entirely and those offended by the poster don't have to look at it.

Forgiveness Really is Divine

Anger is a toxic emotion; it makes people do very stupid and mean things. It makes us blind to others and is the enemy of justice and humanity. If we don't release that anger we can even cause ourselves physical harm. When we are wronged with physical injury, holding onto that anger can even make us immune to healing or other emotions.

When you see the world through a certain perspective and are so angry, you are not receptive to others or what they have to say. It's why people with racist thoughts see racism everywhere, even when it isn't there; or why gays see everything in terms of, was that homophobic, when it was not; or feminists see things as attacks on them – every one of the groups mentioned sees it in terms of black and white, me versus them and any who disagrees is an enemy.

As a culture we have not embraced the idea that letting go of anger and forgiving others might even have health benefits for us. We're encouraged to hold onto anger and not let it go, but the truth is letting go feels really good and can be downright therapeutic. It can be easy to stay angry, especially when we are in the right. It feels more natural to forgive others and move on - like a weight has been lifted and it is like that. Negative emotions cause negative stress, which builds toxins in the body, essentially weighing us down.

Christian Supremacy

It doesn't matter the religion, be it Christian, Pagan, or Muslim, if its tenets preach violence or racial supremacy, it's wrong. The Muslim Brotherhood; the Aryan Nations or white supremacist followers of, Matt Hale, Richard Butler or David Duke; or black supremacist followers of the Churches of Jesse Jackson, Al Sharpton, Jeremiah Wright, Louis Farrakhan, General Yahanna or Yahwen Ben Yahweh, Tom Metzer, or anyone else who think they are better than others.

Chapter **TEN**

UNSKEPTICAL SKEPTICS

Somewhere along the line in the American experiment, we have forgotten the most important way of insuring our freedom - to be skeptical of the government and its related institutions. We should ask more from our government, from our law enforcement, from our media, from our judicial system. Instead of asking these organizations for better behavior we have given them a free pass. Shame on us.

To Neglect and Severe

First off, I want to say there are some really good cops out there, brave men and women who are just trying to help their communities and make society as a whole safer and more civil. They understand the gravity of the promise to protect the citizenry and enforce our nation's laws. They understand that individuals' rights are important and won't violate law abiding citizens' rights of privacy and security.

This segment is not about those officers and I realize that they are put in the middle of all this mess. So I ask them to join in the fight against their comrades who don't feel this way, it's hard to do I'm sure, but your support in this could go a long way.

There's a new piece of legislature out now, to protect all against police misconduct. Officer's uniforms are now outfitted with video cameras, this is definitely a step in the right direction but I have one other suggestion. Before the suggestion, I'm curious as to who has access to this footage? Do they police themselves? Their peers? Their commandeers? See, part of the problem in the past has been the erasing of part of the film. I don't know if that's true or not, but if it is that's a very serious problem. Has this been neutralized? If so, how?

If not here's an idea of how it could be, set up a digital storage system that can't be accessed without a warrant, to store the digital files. To access the video the warrant number has to be used. That's one problem down. Another step would be to reprimand officers who bully those who film them.

In one YouTube video the officer admitted that was harassing the one videoing him to "intimidate" him, but wouldn't have hurt him. Why would he possibly think he might be in danger, a man with a gun on a motorcycle menacingly threatening you why would someone be worried? If they are an honest cop they should not be concerned about having their conduct on film.

They should also not be given more rights than the ordinary citizen; in a court of law their testimony is given more credence. Why? They know the law better than the average citizen and their incentive is to lock up as many people as possible or write the most citations. That's how they advance in their ranks - so how does that give them incentive to enforce the law responsibily? A cop can lay a hand on you without little question of his conduct, but if you try to resist you have committed assault. The one with the superior training in firearms and hand to hand combat and has to maintain a certain level of body conditioning, is also given additional rights by the law. All for doing his job - Wow! Those are quite the perks!

Isn't this a violation of the opening statement of the declaration, "All men are created equal," I get they have a very dangerous job, that voluntarily puts them in harm's way - but granting them these rights has caused men with power to infringe on the rights of those they are supposed to protect!

Understand, not all the blame is on the officers, the system was set up in a manner to reward bad behavior, not good. The more they can use whatever you say against you, the more arrests they make and the sooner they can become that squad commandeer, a private investigator or maybe even a future political office. To change this behavior the system has to change to reward legitimate constitutional legal enforcement techniques. But seeing that doesn't pay as well, as the current Criminal Justice system, I'm not holding my breath.

If the Government is so Right, Why does it use Force?

What I can never wrap my mind around with the liberal mindset is this enormous amount of trust they have in the government. I understand their skepticism of "Big Business", but when it comes to "Big Government" their attitude is - *Oh go ahead do whatever you want. Oh that Constitution, ignore that it's just a dusty old piece of paper anyhow.* Why give the one with the most power even more? Why give up that skepticism for "Big Brother?"

The federal government hasn't made things better; in fact they have to make things inefficient so you will come back for more. People don't go to government when things are working, but when they're not.

There are businesses that operate this way as well, but with all the watchdog organizations and the consumer reporters they are minimized. For a business to scam you is becoming increasingly difficult, but with the left government has been given carte Blanc in all matters.

To be fair this does happen on the right, but not nearly as often or to the same degree. With the market if a product or service is inferior you can move on, but with the government you don't get that option. But if the government was so right why does it limit people to "one size fits all?"

Sleeping Media

Most refer to the encompassing monopoly of the information sources bringing "news" to the public as, the "mainstream media", I prefer to call it the "Sleeping Media" because it's almost like they are in a trance, brought on by "heroic" and "enigmatic" democrats.

The most prized source of the crème de la crème of the outlets, small and large is the *New York Times.* If it's not from the *New York Times*, it's not news!

The obsession with the *New York Times* is kind of odd in the modern era, since the organization is rather antiquated with an obvious liberal bias. It's not exactly a news company with a reputation you should trust and it's without a tangible reason to still be in existence, let alone deserving of the image of the paragon of truth.

It just goes to show that the populists and progressives have and will always be hard at work "interpreting" the world around them.

Conspiracy Theories and Conspiracy Facts

I've always loved reading about conspiracy theories, secret societies, alien connections and mutants spawned from radioactive exposure. As a child I believed the stories as more than fantastic tales, but as absolute truths. As an adult my research has drawn different conclusions.

It should be noted that the conspiracy theories are not like urban legends which are completely made up - conspiracy theories are more legitimate issues of concern that are greatly exaggerated. It also doesn't mean that their existence isn't dangerous.

The idea that we should be skeptical of institutions of society is in fact a smart and proactive step. Conspiracy theories do help foster this, by and large, but its extreme exaggerations also cause people to question their claims, having the side effect that the public ignores the real danger of the possible corruption in these institutions.

The simple fact is the truth doesn't need help in these areas - cronyism is a dangerous concept without involvement of the Freemasons, the birth of the Federal Reserve without need of the Rothschild link, the fluoridation of drinking water is more innocuous than the theorists claim but it's still not right. But all are based on fact.

What's in the Water

You ever hear a conspiracy theory that sounds so absurd you have to look it up to even understand it? That's what this one was for me - Fluoride in the drinking water. I started hearing this and it wasn't that it was inconceivable - that the government was doing it - but the reason for doing it simply didn't jive. The reason stated by the conspiracy theorists was that it was added to make the American public subservient, to turn us all into mindless willing slaves. If that's the case it ain't working.

But the odd thing is that it's partially true. Fluoride is being added to the drinking water supplies in parts of the United States. In grocery stores you see a few brands of bottled water even advertise that fluoride is in their product.

In this case the reason for it is different than what is stated. Fluoride is added as a measure to fight against tooth decay. It's basically big brother acting on your behalf (again) without your say. That is a big problem though, because they are medicating you without your consent. That's a violation of the doctor patient privilege and is still immoral and illegal.

Also there is the potential for a serious health epidemic, since there's no way to monitor what the percentage of fluoride you're getting in your system. That is a valid concern since it is still a poison.

As for the government utilizing this for a mind control technique, doesn't look like that's the case, but this is what I mean by scaring people with embellishments. This is a legitimate concern that is being dismissed because conspiracy theorists would rather try to scare the hell out of everyone than focus on the more "mundane" real story. If they were more honest then more people would say, "this is wrong let's fix it."

Scary Enough without the Rothschild's

In the 1930's a group of capitalists got together on Jeckel Island and sidestepped congress to institute the most powerful monetary behemoth by resurrecting the US Bank, with a new name, The Federal Reserve.

But this isn't scary enough? The Rothschild family needs to be connected to this? For those who are not familiar with the Rothschild family they had massive control of pretty much everything financial during their reign. They were pretty much the mob of their day and nothing happened without their say, conspiracy theorists say things haven't changed.

Problem is there's nothing to link the Rothschild family to the Federal Reserve. The records suggest J.P. Morgan and John Rockefeller are tied to it, but the others participation in the Federal Reserve's inception is not really clear. But the
183

Rothschild scope of influence had died out by then.

The Federal Reserve is real threat and a very concerning prospect, from the original manager to Bernake, it has been the heart of our financial system and a guarded secret immune from scrutiny. The press, the people, the congress, even the president are not allowed to audit it. When pressure has been put on it for transparency, the declaration by the keepers of its secrets is the same - If anyone tries to audit the Fed we will bring down the economy. Putting this degree of power in an entity that even the congress can't exhume isn't scary enough to the conspiracy theorists? It is to me.

Illuminati, Freemasons and Rosicrucians, Oh my!

When I started going through the abundance of conspiracy theory videos on YouTube there was a pattern that emerged, when discussion was on the *New World Order*, it's being brought about by was by the secret societies of the Illuminati, the Freemasons *or* the *Rosicrucians*. There's one big problem with it… there's no evidence of there being a connection of these groups and a *New World Order*, and the what I found to the contrary was far more compelling.

The origins of these fraternities in Europe were in fact not about taking control, but to minimize the cooperation between the Church and the
184

monarchy - they were fighting the theocracies, not enhancing it. The greater the grasp the Church and state co-op got, the harder these secret societies fought back. There's simply no evidence to suggest these groups have even survived to the modern era intact, let alone that they ever tried to overthrough any responsible government - only the authoritarian ones.

But there's evidence of their existence all the time, examples of hand signals by the Hollywood elite and others of power in videos on the internet. What "evidence" there is isn't clear, but I've got a hand signal that's far clearer for the conspiracy theorists - but they won't like it! If random vague "hand signals" and the close-up of eyes in pictures of magazines is your "proof", sorry guys you're reading into something that's not there.

The societies that are causing so much harm aren't so secret; they hide right out in the open. ACORN, the EPA (pretty much any government organization for that matter), Moveon.org, Media Matters, MSNBC, the Open Society Foundation, OWN, the NEA, unions, lobbyists, special interest groups and the ACLU, all are more dangerous than these "secret societies" are - and they hope you pay attention to the Illuminati, so you will ignore the genuine dangerous societies that operate right out in the open.

And the Winner is...

Probably the all-time weirdest and most outlandish conspiracy theory is one that states NASA has proof that our earth has a planetary doppelganger (evil twin) Nibiru or more commonly *Planet X*, that will collide with our planet and destroy it.

As absurd as this may sound even this has some truth to it. It has to do with the irregular orbits of certain planets in other solar systems. These planets cross into the orbits of other more massive planets and their gravity flings the smaller planet into open space - turning it into basically a massive asteroid.

Is it possible that one of these projectile planets could cross our path? If so, could it destroy our planet? Yes, on both but that's just one of the possible disaster scenario outcomes.

Another is that even if it doesn't strike the planet if it's gravity is power enough it could disrupt earth's orbit, maybe throwing it off balance or if the other invading planet is larger it could even send earth out into open space.

Asteroids and these migratory planets are not the only threats to our planet, though.

If our solar system crosses close enough to another solar system, we could get hit by the radiation and heat of one of its stars. Or it's gravity or the gravity of a planet larger than earth or a black hole in that system.

Pulsar stars or Neutron stars could radiate our planet from light years away.

A migratory black hole could invade our solar system causing chaos in our neighborhood of the universe, before it rips the earth apart. There are so many destructive forces in the universe and they are migratory it seems and at some point we could be reminded that as far as the universe is concerned we are a grain of sand on a grain of sand.

Statistics: The Ultimate Lie

When political commentators find themselves with a lack of evidence to support their claim, but they don't want to admit it, there is one more tool in their toolbox - the statistic, but how valid are statistics? In a lot of cases, not very.

Let's start with the one used the most often, the graft chart, a line that shows whether the number of people affected or product or service uses goes up or down, during a certain time period. OSHA, for example has held up a graft chart to validate the organization's benefit to society - using it to demonstrate that work injuries have gone down, since its founding. That falls apart however, when you look at the same chart from thirty or forty years earlier - because the work related injuries were going down anyway, after OSHA came along the decline stopped and stayed at a steady level. How many other government agencies are like this?

Now let's proceed to another "funny math" trick of the federal government, the budget. At the end of the Clintonian era, we ended with a surplus - or did we? To understand the trick you have to

187

understand how the government economics works, see the government borrows money from another country - mostly China - and uses that to pay for its massive budget and what's left over, is a surplus. So, it's not a real surplus, but more of an unspent loan.

Another trick that has been used by the current administration is the use of duplicate programs, if you go to WhiteHouse.gov and check out the CBO budget report for 2012, you will see most of the "cuts" were of programs that were instituted the last year and duplicates.

These actions are expected by the government and statistics in the free market models don't have this problem, do they? Yes, it does happen, especially by the sleeping media. The pollsters will take the results and find arbitrary reasons to not count all the results - the results, that would disprove their claims, or they might only poll in areas with a high turn-out of the desired results.

So, they get the results they desired, even though the general public might be against the policy by and large. *Rasmussen* has been reported as the most honest and reliable polling system, and one poll is very interesting and telling in its results - that the attitudes of the general public are basically polar opposite of the political elite. We needed a poll to figure that out?

Chapter **ELEVEN**

UNCONVENTIONAL THOUGHTS

The best way to combat Conventional Wisdom is with commonsense. Like the logic in observing what is actually going on before making a judgment. Or trying to foster equality, not create it. Or not spending money that is the general publics frivolously. Or that remembering that "We the People" are the ones who actually have the power.

A Not so Happy Birthday, America!

In step with the typical IRS idiocy (or that of most government agencies for that matter), the belt tightening is being done in areas where the benefit would be for the people, so they can continue spending where it is best for the IRS.

In this case, it's the July 4th celebrations on military bases. To try to pacify those of us who advocate and push for fiduciary responsibility with regards to public funds - in their wisdom - the IRS pulled the pyrotechnic displays. The costs of the fireworks, it should be mentioned, was only $50,000.

This might seem like the right move on the part of the IRS, but this is out of the proper context.

First, of all this is but a comparatively minor amount of a bloated budget and is another clear sign of reckless regard of the public financial trust.

Second, the fireworks display is for the publics' advantage. The other programs listed are not.

Third, this is a once a year expense in the federal tally sheet. But this is a larger problem being made evident here - the lack of respect for the public's desire of where *their money* should be spent. Obviously, your tax dollars should not be spent on garish parties and lavish gifts, for companies to buy their favor, but that's where it's going.

Another piece of *Unconventional Thought* is this, that it's part of a concise agenda to eliminate the 4th of July. The death of Independence Day would make the agenda of the end of independence itself that much easier.

A Fair Trade-Off

So the other day I was killing time before a work meeting, I went to check for any worthwhile deals at one of the discount stores. At the clearance section I happened upon a shirt marked .49. Looking through the rest of the rack I found other shirts marked $6.49, so I thought that my find was simply tagged wrong. But at only 50 cents what's a few minutes.

So I looked around a little bit longer, but didn't find anything else. When checking out there was a long line greeting me. Right before me was a very impatient woman, who was eager to voice her dissatisfaction about having to wait. Okay, J-Lo relax.

First she takes her case to her fellow shoppers, then to the cashier. Her favorite criticism was *"This is not good business practices, leaving the customers to wait for 15 minutes."* The wait has closer to half that time, but putting that aside I started pondering the validity of her argument. I have a combined ten years' experience in retail, so I do have some understanding about retail economics. If she had been in retail, she had forgotten what it was like, but I held my tongue because this was none of my business. The fact is unless you have worked in customer service, you have no idea just how stressful it can be. Now that doesn't mean all employees (or management, for that matter) are always right, but then again neither is the customer.

See the business practices the manager utilized there is an efficient and practical one for that particular retail niche. If the discount stores started employing more people, or even increased the hours of the current employees work, the management would have to mark up their prices. So that cartful of products in your cart, that you're getting for about seventy dollars at the discount store might cost you THREE HUNDRED at a regular retail store. That's what people don't think of.

Anyway, back to the lady. The other error on her part was who she was complaining to. First, the other patrons of the store, then the cashier. I've seen this before, they think that they can garner support from the other shoppers, but the fact is they are being a roadblock to the others and who is going to side with a roadblock. Besides, what exactly are they hoping to accomplish with this anyway? A kind of shopper rebellion? Making them who - *William Wallace*?

Let's be real about her intention here, this was not about actually voicing the complaint, but about making a point. If her purpose was settling a grievance, than she would have asked the cashier to call the manager. The cashier can't do anything; she's just trying to make a living. She also shouldn't have whined to the other shoppers. She made the choice to be an irritant rather than evaluating the situation for more constructive solutions. She could have left the line and continued shopping until the line had shrunk, or left and come back later, or simply left, for good.

Point is if she had her way, she and all the rest of us there would have had to pay more for the products we were getting. She got the products for a fraction of the market value price, at a cost of a few extra minutes (which since this is a unpredictable variable, she might have still had to spend those extra few minutes at one of the more expensive stores) and I got my shirt for a grand total of .52 with tax. I think that tradeoff is pretty fair.

Passing the Bill

Have you ever looked at the list of items you can write-off on your taxes as deductions? If you set up your own business, there's pretty much nothing that can't be written off - it's the percentage that can be the question.

If a computer is used for both business and personal uses only about 50% of the cost can be deducted, but it is still deductible. Any supplies related to your business is open for deduction, printers, phones, computers, I-Pads, furniture, TVs, advertising costs - if you can prove it's legitimate, you're free to add it to your list of deductions.

Even with all this "open for interpretation" philosophy, people still try to sneak absurd deductions on their taxes - like getting a speedboat when you have an office job, not a reasonable deduction; or a helicopter, when you have to hire a pilot and your clientele are all local to your business, a very *un*reasonable deduction.

This is the world of tax write-offs, it transforms businessmen into freeloaders, I know because I'm one too! As the sole proprietor and owner of MOJO Publishing I'm a business freeloader, taking advantage of the tax system. But businesses do a lot to improve our lives and with all the fluster and puffing up about the "evils of business and corporate greed", the government offers all businesses certain tax breaks and in blind faith, that the act will be an "investment" and the businesses will spend more money which helps the economy.

For the most part it does work, but it would work far better without all the regulations that hurt businesses by bleeding them dry. Even being someone who does take advantage of it, I do know the tax code does need simplification though, much to the chagrin of the tax attorneys out there. Starting off with the elimination of the income tax and going to a flat tax instead, plus maybe we can finally end the absurdity about the class warfare assertions. No one will be taxed on income so policy discussions that include pandering to the "class warfare" extremists would be ridiculous - oh what a wonderful world that would be.

Little Acts of Treason

When the incident with Bradley Manning first made headlines, my initial reaction was this - I felt that his actions could be construed as treasonous, because the source he divulged his information to - Wikileaks and Julian Assange, who was perceived as having anti-American tendencies and was looking to embarrass

193

the nation, and it didn't sit well with me that Manning was getting paid.

After reconsidering the situation my opinion changed: he put his life in harm's way and had to flee the country, so maybe compensation for it was acceptable and Wikileaks was not as anti-American as originally thought, but portrayed that way by those who gained in minimizing the whole issue. It was Assange's involvement that made me uncomfortable, but that might have been his only option and the reason my view changed was because of Edward Snowden. Snowden, I never saw as a traitor; he gave an oath to protect and defend the constitution, against all enemies - foreign *and domestic*; the basic principle of the document, is to protect the people from the government, in order to preserve it that he had no other choice *but* to release that information. That was his duty to the American people.

The reply from the Obama administration, of branding him a possible traitor, is typical to his view of whistleblowers; according to researchers he has prosecuted more informants and journalists than any other president. This is the same old story, of the king declaring a hero to be a traitor - because he dares to stand up against the crown.

Truth leads to Truth

At the time of its invention the polygraph was

considered to be the greatest tool in law enforcement - taking away the claims of bias by law officers. The machine operates by monitoring the suspect's vital signs; increases in breathing, sweating, heart rate, etc., and alerts the operator of the changes. There's a major problem that in the system that can't be neutralized - the physical stresses are not necessarily because of guilt, but from the situation.

With the polygraph it could be the stress of a false positive and going to jail, with the original interrogation techniques used by law enforcement prior to the polygraph and still used today - it's a system of intimidation used to wear down the suspect into confessing. What you're not told is that you can leave at any time and you don't have to talk to the officers. If you're not formerly arrested, they can't stop you from leaving.

In interviews with people who have falsely confessed they tell of the mental exhaustion that is used - being lied to and told you're guilty and they can prove it, for hours on end. Here's a tip: If they could prove it, they   would have already charged you. The mentally handicapped are especially vulnerable to this, since they are eager to please authority figures.

There are even cases when the police have been proven to have fed suspects information on the case to charge them. This was discovered in the case of suspected serial killer, Henry Lee Lucas, apparently the overly enthusiastic officers told Lucas and his cohort details that "only the killer could know" to get them for a series of murders. The only link to Lucas on more than a couple of the murders was his confession and his knowledge of the where the victims were discovered, no physical evidence of Lucas' presence before then was found but there was evidence pointing to the fact the two men were not involved. Lucas and his accomplice retracted their confessions to the other crimes and said the police gave them the tips of the crimes.

So, why did they go along with it? The duo had had run ins with the police and wanted to embarrass the department.

Another problem that can occur with both the polygraph and police interrogations, what if the suspect doesn't see what they did as wrong? They are dealing with sociopaths after all and their views are not the same about the value of human life. One man's murder could be another's getting rid of "undesirables."

Mr. Rogers did it

The most successful bank robbers will be the ones who go in with a suit and tie and are clean shaved. Why? Because that's what most people trust blindly, there's even a scientific theory about, called the "*Halo Effect.*"

Changing parts of the face, even slightly, will make for a very alien appearance, which is why the robotic technology we have now has its limits on advancement - they still look like a Barbie doll.

So, how does all this apply to our society and the discussion? It has very dangerous implications with the before mentioned bank robber scenario, which is actually the most benign of all the possibilities. This blind trust has had very traumatic consequences to society, with victims ranging from those conned with simple street scams to being found deceased.

Think of it like this, how many of the world's serial killers and mass murderers looked like a homeless beggar and of lesser intelligence and how many were instead like the boy next door? The answer, most were clean-cut young men with a strong direction in life - the kind that momma would try to set up her daughter with. Only a few exceptions to this have occurred - Charles Manson and John Wayne Gacy, to name a couple, but even Gacy was non-threatening, which is what they wanted. Look as "normal" as possible to lull the populace into a sense of unskeptical trust.

This also encourages their victims to ignore their extreme eccentricities until it's too late. Add to this mixture their aura of authority; they have made themselves a very effective "wolf in sheep's" clothing.

Too Much Television

If you ask people if they think TV shows have gone too far, in regards to violence, sex and language, and it's causing the moral decay of society - many will say, yes. I doubt that though, but find it rather surprising the people who make this claim, come to this conclusion. How is this conclusion any different from the claim that a *YouTube* video caused the attack and deaths of the Americans in Benghazi?

Both claims abdicate the responsibility for the individuals involved and place it on the art of the culture - this is scapegoating. The claim of cultural art causing moral decay is nothing new, and the excessive sex and violence on TV is not a recent cultural shift but part of a slow process. Since the invention of television, there have always been shows that have pushed the limits and there have always been critics to scream they have exceeded the boundaries of decency.

One of the earliest examples of this is the classic show, *I Love Lucy. I Love Lucy,* was controversial? In its era it was *very* controversial, starting with the couple themselves... an interracial couple. A Cuban immigrate and a white native New Yorker, a married couple - it might happen, but it's certainly was a provocative situation and made the show's producers extremely worried.

It also covered issues real couples deal with the unabashed honest never seen before, including for the first time... the bedroom, despite the fact they slept in twin beds, it was still considered a gutsy move. Then a new problem came up, Lucy Ball got pregnant - that would mean the end of the show, but not to Lucy or husband Desi and no to canceling the show. The show didn't simply make an episode to announce the event - but the entire pregnancy
198

through-out the season.

What about violence and blood on TV, surely that wasn't on the classic shows. I guess you didn't watch enough of the origin *Twilight Zone* from the 1960's, as well as being a brilliant satire; it also had occasional scenes of violence which did end in bloodshed. The episode "*The Monsters are Due on Maple Street*" has a scene with one of the actors with a nasty head wound with a trail of blood.

The show was a pioneer in the fact that it took on social issues, such as the Holocaust, nuclear war and discrimination. It was socially important and it was honest, which is why its violations of cultural norms were ignored.

Well, what about homosexuality? That didn't get addressed until the 1990's; did you forget about the shows *MASH, All in the Family* or *Three's Company?* All three covered homosexuality, *All in the Family* and *MASH* dealt with other social issues as well. They both added obscenities and vulgar racial terms to TV shows, *MASH* also added violence and in one episode a nude scene (it happens really fast, but it is there).

But the movies now-a-days are so extreme - as opposed to say, Alfred Hitchcock's classics? When Hitchcock's classic *Psycho*, was originally released it was before the rating code was developed afterwards it got an R rating, it was pretty intense but it was really bloody. Many dismiss that because it was in black and white and it's well known they used chocolate syrup for an analog for blood - so they used chocolate syrup for blood, they use corn syrup with red dye for blood in modern times - doesn't change the fact that it was violent and had blood in it.

Then there's the original *Planet of the Apes*, which has comparatively a lot of nudity in it, but the whole series is pretty bloody as well.

Now, you may have noticed a pattern developing in the examples mentioned that most of them are from the sixties and seventies, a time famous in American history for a cultural acceptance of openly questioning our social institutions. The operative word here is "openly" questioned, the social norms were being debated in previous decades, as early as thirty years earlier- during the 1930's the focus as on WWII, so all this was over-shadowed.

The legislature of Franklin Roosevelt were paramount to the sixties social revolutions, but he didn't encourage the openness of the sixties. He even had laws in place that you couldn't criticize the war effort, but Roosevelt was all about censorship - so all this shouldn't be a surprise. Eleanor Roosevelt was a perfect match, since she was as big a progressive as Franklin and was reported to being a bisexual with a lesbian partner - she actually started the homosexual agenda in the thirties and forties, before the sixties radicals.

Changes in technology will always bring out those who will break the models of convention, but considering convention seems to be more about hiding the truth of the evolving alterations of society - I think the openness is a welcome change of pace.

Cookie Cutter Solutions don't Work

This is a nation of entrepreneurs, those who aren't afraid to step out on a limb, to reach for the brass ring and improve the lives of themselves and their families and the lives of others whom they employ as well. Some would argue that the best system are the ones that work for all, I would contest that this is not only untrue, but also an impossibility.

This is the trap of what I call the "Cookie-Cutter" system model. A unified, unrealistic philosophy that simply doesn't apply to the real world model.

Everyone is different down to the molecular level. We are in the simplest terms, the output of two separate genetic codes interwoven after all. A series of biological ones and zeroes from our parent's DNA, mutating and creating unique deviations or deformities. In humans this (along with environment and our individual experiences) transforms into our moral code, which is what most of us use to guide our decisions for the rest of our lives.

Because of the existence of this moral code is the reason that the "Cookie-Cutter" system can't work. What our reactions to a given situation are is not inevitable, it's at best an educated guess based on past interactions with the person. The point is we make choices, financial, moral, and spiritual, that is the part of the equation under our control, anyway. Then there are outside factors that are out of our control, that's the other part of the equation.

In conclusion, the human will towards liberty is too strong and such attempts to circumvent your will on someone else, is sure to end in their favor. The larger point here is that not only trying to make decisions of how others should live as unlikely, but it's also ethically wrong. Setting up a system based on this model is like trying to cage up a hurricane.

The Family Farm is the Safest Place

Engrained in the psyche of the American mindset is this nostalgia of the family farm - the warm feeling from the Norman Rockwell utopia, that it's an icon of independence and safety.

In modern times the former is far from true with the farm and agricultural industries being one of the largest federal subsidy schemes, making the traditional "family farm", being a thing of the past. Now the farming that takes place is done by the government.

As for the latter, that has never been as true as people want to believe and our perception of security has more to do with the sentimentality to the family farm. The safest social structure to live in is in the suburbs, middle to high end apartments or condominiums. Big cities are only dangerous because of the high number of the populace in a single area, but proportionally it's not any less safe than living in a smaller town.

In a small town what makes it less safe is the there's less people and the isolation, this makes these areas *more* inviting for criminals. Many residents of small towns keep firearms, but there are a lot of large cities that are still open for gun ownership too. The claim of the safety associated with the "family farm" is only as true as the individual makes it - but it's not really any safer, since the points proponents advance are in fact what make it a more calculated risk.

We are Here to Say Goodbye to Mr. Sprinkles

Have you ever heard of the company *Peternity?* It's a company with the mission of helping pet owners with the difficult and emotionally draining experience of having a pet die and how to remember them.

Being a pet owner myself - a list that has included different species of reptiles, invertebrates, amphibians and exotic fish, as well as the more traditional dog - it's a very emotional experience. You get just as attached to snake or frog, as a cat or dog and it's not easy to say goodbye and it feels like you're losing a family member.

While humanizing a pet, such as a large dog or large snakes or exotic cats, can have dangerous consequences in the lives of the community if the animal gets loose since it has lost its fear of man - grieving in ways that are similar to the funeral arrangements we make for our parents is nothing that we should feel ashamed for. Those who have never kept any pets won't understand this, but the manner in which you grieve is none of their business.

That's why *Peternity* was created; to help

those who can't let go will always have a part of their beloved pet forever. Some of the products and services offered by this industry even I find unorthodox and don't necessarily agree with but if it's what you feel comfortable with, that's for you to decide. Go ahead and get that tattoo that has Spot's ashes mixed with the ink, or stuff Fluffy and have her curled up by the fireplace, or if you can afford it throw Mr. Sprinkles a full funeral with casket.

Whatever helps you deal with the loss of a loyal friend is up to you, and I'm sorry for your loss.

Hey Bartender

"It's just sad to see him at drinking at home all alone..." that's the conventional wisdom, but how wise is it really? Basically, it's telling those who want to drink to the point of forgetting that day, that they should get out of the house, drive to the bar and then drive back.

If their goal is to get completely tanked instead of having a couple of drinks to relax from a hard day, staying at home and not putting others in harm's way seems like a better attitude to encourage. Go ahead be your own bartender, and then we will have one less statistic to scrape off the asphalt.

Another plus for the one doing the drinking at home - it's comparatively cheaper, since the drinks won't be watered down. Bars and other such places are where you go to socialize and recuperate, not a place to go get plastered - so, let's change our social common consensus and tell them it's better for them to stay at home and hurt themselves, than to go to the bar and hurt others driving home drunk.

Can't Even Make an Al Gore Joke Anymore

I hate getting into political conversations with friends, they never go well. Especially when it's online, it's so hard to express tone and mine is usually fairly sarcastic but online who can tell. There were two conversations that were particularly horrendous.

In the first one here's what happened - I was going through *YouTube* videos and I came across one with an aspiring Governor running in Nevada, who made the statement that when he gets the job he would start proceedings into the impeachment of president Obama.

I reposted this video on one of the social media sites stating that, *"If I ever become a Nevada state resident I would vote for him."* Admittedly it was a flippant remark and not a critical analysis, and I didn't thoroughly investigate the governor. For the most part I liked what he said in this video and since he was running as a Constitutionalist party candidate, there was a good chance I would for the most part agree with him.

Anyway, a dear friend of mine approached me on where he stands on the issues so I went to his website and copied and pasted a reply on the relevant issues. Namely healthcare reform, since I knew they had a serious ailment that would be the topic of discussion even before they said it. I ended the conversation stating that I agreed with the governor that healthcare reform is better left to the states and that a federal mandate for this, like most issues I don't support.

The other noted conversation had to do with the temporary re-re-re-revitalization of Al Gore's career with his enviro-activism. The heading in the *Washington Times* was *"Republicans secretly tell Al Gore they are worried about Climate Change,"* after writing a little snippet on the original post, I reposted this with my own comment,

"Why do the global warming crowd still hold up Al Gore as a keystone figure of the movement? His antics have hurt more than helped them. The empirical evidence shows that climate change is perfectly normal and natural, and the human race is unnoticed by the planet. If I were in the eco- conspiracy crowd though, I would take away Gore's decoder ring and show him the door!"

This comment didn't go unchallenged; another casual observation bites the dust! Basically another friend in this case had contention with the "unnoticed" line in the post. Which I do stand behind and was trying to get across that what I have read has led me to be skeptical of the green movements underlining agenda.

In the end this too was concluded at a point of no resolution. Why? Well a couple of reasons, both my remarks were casual, satirical comments made in the moment and not what I felt strongly enough to defend. This is not the only time I've had to do this and have held my own fine before.

The other and more important reason why this was different was because they were both friends of mine. Not just online friends, but people that I had a real association with. One was a high school friend and the other was a woman I had previous dated and kept in touch with.

Even before these encounters I had had to deal with this from my former roommate from time to time. When you get into these debates with people whose opinion you care about or you didn't know they felt that way it will steamroll you and can really throw you off. When alert and fully able to articulate the point with clear concise arguments its one thing, otherwise it's simply a headache and not enjoyable in the slightest. So the best piece of advice on this, don't start a debate with a friend unless you're sure about it and keep it on the down low instead of online.

Chapter **TWELVE**

BLOOMBERGISM:
BLUEPRINT FOR OPPRESSION

This is a bonus chapter I just had to add, about every libertarian's favorite authoritarian, New York Mayor Michael Bloomberg.

Contra-bottle

Mayor **Michael Bloomberg** of New York, has conceived some of the most peculiar, tyrannical laws that he deserves his own chapter of this book - his campaign against the baby bottle is a first-rate example of why. This act was actually one of the reasons that I wrote this book, I couldn't even begin to fathom what he was thinking.

In the hospitals of New York, if a mother gives birth and wants to feed her child, she still has the option of either breastfeeding or bottle-feeding her child - if she chooses the bottle, she has to ask for it and endure a lecture by the nurses, about the benefits of breast milk. If after the lecture she's still so stubborn (or too exhausted) she wants to get the baby the bottle - that troublemaker her - then the nurse will have to get the key to unlock the cabinet where the contraband bottle is kept. That's right; the baby bottles are under lock and key.

Yes, because I'll bet they get a lot of mothers sneak in and bust out the bottles with a crowbar; or maybe they wear a ski-mask and hold the nurses at gunpoint - give me all your baby bottles and formula, and no one will get hurt.

Big Brother on Steroids

When most people think about the idea of the story *1984* turning into a reality, they get a sense of dread - not our friend Mr. Bloomberg, he gets the warm feeling that he should be getting for Christmas. He wants video cameras on every street corner, drones flying over-head and the massive police force, keeping New Yorkers into submission... Okay, the last one I don't know about, but with this little despot anything is possible. The rest is true though, he wants every citizen of New York to have cameras trained on them.

The odd thing in the story is when the proposal of equipping the policemen was brought up in other states, he hated the idea - apparently he doesn't care if the police use excessive force or if police brutality records are high in the big apple, as long he can control the masses.

Dr. Pepper, Big Macs and Electronic Cigarettes

Bloomberg has been one of the biggest supporters of the Obama agendas: the health Gestapo policies and the police state expansions, but he has even come up with ideas the president hasn't thought of, giving them state models to go by.

The War on the 64 Ozer, for a brief history in New York the 64 oz. bottle of soda was considered contraband - fortunately, the state supreme court had the good sense to see this as an infringement on choice, calling the bans *"arbitrary and capricious."* This is not the end of it vowed Bloomberg, and in reply stated his health policies have *"helped New Yorkers live longer, healthier lives,"* who cares if they have to give up their personal liberties in the process. In his efforts to further invade New Yorkers diets he has been more than happy to jump on the bandwagon with the president's fight against trans-fat, making it mandatory for both chains, such as: Subway, Burger King, McDonald's and New Yorkers local fixtures, to post their calorie counts. To further argue the need for these measures, Bloomberg argues *"life expectancy in our city is now 3 years longer than in 2001 and more than 2 years than the national average."* Wow! - 2 whole years longer! Sorry, but the payoffs don't seem substantial enough to warrant this intrusion.

To get the full picture of his health extreme concepts we have to analyze his battle with tobacco, he's one of the few ardent critics against the electronic cigarettes market. Even with the alternatives to smoking Bloomberg isn't happy, he clearly won't be satisfied unless there's no smoking in New York. With his *"Sensible Tobacco Enforcement Law,"* he claims to be effectively curtailing youth smoking, by raising the age to purchase cigarettes to 21 and ending the discounted and untaxed cigarettes sales. Not all New Yorkers like the law, according the Health Commissioner, Thomas A. Farley, *"the number of retailers flouting the law has reached an epidemic level..."* The proposed solution to this is to increase the price to $10.50 a pack - good idea, penalize those who legally buy the product, by making it the highest price. That will end the black markets, by giving them *more* business.

If Bloomberg had written the Controlled Substances Act, instead of Franklin Roosevelt, it would have included: soda, all forms of tobacco, fast food and baby formula.

Another Green Goon

As well as jumping on the generic left wing health policies, Bloomberg is a hardcore environmentalist, with a ban on Styrofoam cups stating *"we know [the cups] are environmentally destructive,"* and in 2007 he proposed an $8.00 penalty for driving your own car in Manhattan, calling it a "congestion charge" - I call it environmental idiocy. This is only a fraction of his environmental tyranny; the most extreme green programs have to do with the efforts to rebuild after coastal storms - he argues for his "resiliency projects" with this statement -

"All across our city - and especially in the coastal communities that Hurricane Sandy hit so hard - we're making strides on many fronts toward one goal: Protecting New Yorkers against major coastal storms or extreme weather events.... we've mapped out a strategy for.... a comprehensive resiliency plan. It includes 257 separate initiatives to strengthen our
211

coast lines, protecting our critical infrastructure…. it's a far-reaching $20 billion plan."

Don't get me wrong, spending to rebuild is acceptable and necessary - but what New Yorkers should be asking is, where and how he's spending that money? Another point, New York is one of the oldest states in the country, why don't they have an emergency fund?

Part of Bloomberg's green agenda, is to increase the government housing in New York. He's using a multifamily building repair program - *Built it Back* - to accomplish this, *Knickerbocker Village,* one of the state supervised affordable housing developments recently received $46 million.

He also set up an effort to clean up 7,600 acres of brownfields in the city, that's great, but I have to ask - who's doing the clean-up, a private corporation, or another agency established by Bloomberg for the effort? Another initiative of Bloomberg, is to convert 13,000 taxis to hybrids cars, he obviously hasn't done his research on hybrids - making the battery for one of these cars, *exponentially increases* greenhouse gasses - now times that by 13,000. The Bloomberg green agenda is looking like it's even more flawed than his health initiatives, at least the health policies - while draconian - had logical weight to them.

And the Madness Continues

How does rummaging through your refuse to make sure your food is put in the proper bin, grab you?

That's what Mr. Bloomberg's newest idea is for the metropolitan utopia. It actually strikes me as funny really, thinking about the residents of one of the most refined cities in the world - having to make sure their disposed food stuffs are placed in the proper bins.

This could be the most stupid thing; I've ever heard of - *Food Recycling*, Bloomberg really is a lunatic!

The Most Dangerous Man in the United States

This is the statement made by Glenn Beck - that Michael Bloomberg is "*the most dangerous man in the United States*"; I do agree with Mr. Beck on this, but for a different reason, Beck stated that with Bloomberg's money and ideology that makes him very dangerous. That's a good reason, the affluent can greatly influence legislature, but that's not the only way Bloomberg is dangerous - but he also sets what I call the "Blueprint for Oppression."

The "Blueprint for Oppression", is the policies he set forth could give an ambitious young dictator, new and inventive forms of authoritarian rules before unheard of. That's what makes him "the most

213

dangerous man in the United States" for me. From his fight against New Yorkers choice of consumables - such as, fast food, sodas and cigarettes (even e-cigarettes that only cause harm to the smoker). To his intervention into New Yorker's health choices with the "Contra-bottle" policy. To his over the top food recycling and his version of the Orwellian security state with cameras on every corner (except on the police, where the cameras should be). To his unrelenting war on guns.

Fortunately, his *Mayors against Guns* campaign become a party of one and the other mayors bowed out. One bad policy down in the Big Apple, but far too many are left.

The states are considered places of government experimentation, to see which policies work on the small scale - it appears with someone like Bloomberg in control, we have seen the way to the legislative *Frankenstein's Monster!*

Light at the End of the Tunnel

Bloomberg's stifling oppression isn't fooling everyone, one example is the legislature changes by Mississippi Governor Phil Bryant, who signed a bill referred to as the "anti-Bloomberg" bill. The basic principle of the law prevents municipalities from governing what or how much people can eat and drink.

Bryant's statement when signing the bill, "It is simply not the role of government to micro-regulate citizens' dietary decisions. The responsibility for one's personal health depends on individual choices about a proper diet and appropriate exercise." Finally a politician who gets it! He understands what his duty is and backed laws that protect his constituency against the Bloombergism philosophy. Bryant understands how important choices are for the people - if we get more political figures who endorse anti-Bloomberg laws, then liberty could return.

Blueprint for Oppression

If everything else mentioned, his inept green policies, his health Gestapo, his food recycling, his extensive security measures, or his battle against tobacco or guns; isn't enough, here are a few more of his policies that invade New Yorkers rights or create a false equality for designated demographics - such as the moronic notion of supporting the building of a mosque near Ground Zero. They can do it - it's just not a bright idea, and shows how truly insensitive the "tolerant and sensitive" left-wing progressives really are.

Another cause of Bloomberg is using DNA and fingerprinting technology to create a worker database, yeah, a totalitarian should be trusted with that! There's also his *Pay-for-Prevention* program, which is really nothing more than indoctrination for the universal coverage initiative.

To be fair, there are programs that he approves of that I agree with - he supports immigration and free trade, for example - but, all in all Bloomberg is a dangerous man, because he has a lot of money, but more because he has given the world the updated version of the *Blueprint for Oppression.*

Conclusions **AND SOLUTIONS**

Now how do we fix these problems? Well, here are my suggestions.

Federalism has Failed

In the *Americanus Libertae* School of Political Science and Popular Culture Studies, when it comes to our government's intervention and federalism - it gets an F. Everything that has been touched by the government has been infested with corruption. Let's go down the list:

Education- A system of propaganda, which hides the truth. It advances the idea that morality is irrelevant and as long as your actions have "good intentions", the ends justify the means. The system instructs what to think not how to think. The danger to humanity is extremely high. Failure!

Environmental Issues- There is potential for good in this area, but the movement has been absorbed by ideologues, more interested in creating a machine for control. Manipulation has been used to advance the Overpopulation theory and has ties in sterilization, genocide, eugenics and is unrealistic to the needs of the real world, ignoring economic theories. It has already caused damage. Failure!

Welfare- With modern technological advances, including internet jobs, the existence of the welfare program on every level is debatable. As is, the program has more to do with placing more of the populace in a position of government dependency,

217

than assisting those in need - rewarding those with a lack of ambition and penalizing the ones in need of temporary aid. It kills jobs because of its high monetary incentives for little or no work output, and is a burden to the taxpayer. Its damage to morale and the economy is long standing. Failure!

Healthcare- Medicare and Medicaid have kept the costs of treatments inflated due to a lack of competition. The next step the Affordable Care Act, takes that to the next level. Even now, prior to its full implementation it has proven destructive to the economy, encouraging employers to maintain as minimal a staff as possible and at part time only. Franchises and small and local businesses are going to be hurt the most, since they still have to comply with the regulations of the power house companies with a far smaller customer base due to demographic. Many companies have already down-sized or closed down completely since the ACA was announced, many more will be lost after its regulations go into effect. The other point of consideration is the bills size- over 2,000 pages, there's a lot of rules that have nothing to do with Healthcare. Its possibilities for good are far less than its negative outcome for society. Failure- and the worst is yet to come!

Quantative Easing- Unnecessary and invasive, the economy is mixed by free markets and recovers faster without government assistance. Failure!

Bailouts- The industries bailed out still have poor management and need a housecleaning. A venture
218

capitalist firm would have put the companies in a stronger position without all the waste. Bailouts don't fix the inefficiencies, but swipe them under the rug, so they managerial ineptitude come return with a vengeance. No company is too big to fail. Failure, through non-failure!

*City Bailouts- Same as the company bailouts. Detroit recently has been bailed out at the cost of $320 million. Failure, threw not learning!

*Border Security- Nonexistent, but expensive. The border fence will never be built, yet the nation spends billions on it. Failure, through bad policies!

*Morality Enforcement- Morality laws come at a high cost- billions of dollars annually and are very ineffective. Morality laws have caused moral decay. Failure, in every possible way!

*Corporatism- Under the call for restrictions on corporate welfare queens, many have given the government full discretion on inhibitions on the large corporations. This has been used by government representatives to provide favors and bribes to their friends in the corporate world. This method of ending corporatism has backfired, because it gives those who set up the defective rules to begin with more authority. A system that empowers the general public is the only way to fix this. EPIC Failure!

All these policies have one commonality, with the exception of border security, that the government has no real constitutional authority in any of these matters. Even on the matters that the government does have the right to weigh in, have been failures, and just because they can intervene doesn't mean they should.

The constitution gives the congress authority to establish a post office, maintain a secure border and to coin money. The president to appoint judges, but that's basically it. All these programs are full of waste and cronyism, and could be done better by the open market. The post offices across the country would do better with less - the smaller ones would be closed under the free market. That would be a lot of saved revenue and no waste.

Border security is a constitutional right granted to the government, but the system they made is flawed. Bring the troops home and place them across the border would be a better enforcement technique, or give this to the states to sort out for themselves. That sounds like a scary idea, but most anti-federalist concepts do - that doesn't make it the wrong way to go!

Congress has abdicated their right to coin money a long time ago, by granting it to the Federal Reserve - they need to reclaim it somehow. We also need to return to the gold standard if possible. Bitcoin has excellent possibilities as it was set up by the open market, as long as everyone keeps an eye on it for government influence, but so far it's a definite plus for capitalism. Options such as Bitcoin could put the economy back into the hands of the people.

As for the courts and judges, the lifetime appointments for judges was a good idea, but has had bad side effects. If no reasonable solution is reached to neutralize the judges that have strayed from constitutional grounds in their rulings, abolishment of the lifetime appointment may need to be considered. Term limits put fear back into our representatives of the different branches of government. Maybe then the judges will put more thought into the cases they accept.

Federalism has not only failed the people, the people have failed by letting its government run amuck. It's not too late though, but we as a nation have tough choices to make things better.

Do Prohibitions Really Work

After reading this book, here's the question - do prohibitions really work? Put aside your emotional or moral objection for a moment and evaluate this logically, the effectiveness of making morals and ethics a subject to legal statutes is very much debatable proposal.

Prohibiting behaviors that inflict physical harm - if you steal or destroy another's property; or if you violate another person's body; or if you take a gun to work and go on a shooting spree, you give up your rights to be a member of civil society - but what if the gun is used on yourself instead, should that be a crime? Yes, suicide is immoral, but should it really be illegal? Okay, the gun has a problem that it could harm others as well, but what about taking a bunch of pills.

You're causing physical harm to yourself and emotional harm to your loved ones, but not to society itself, so why is this a crime? I'm not advocating suicide, but asking how this is a *federal issue*? Let's expand this scenario one more time and say you have an incurable disease, that you know will be extremely painful and you don't want to suffer - shouldn't that be between you and your doctor, and not the feds? We have *Do Not Resuscitate* orders, why not *Do Not Infringe* orders? It's easy to take a stand against this when you're not the one walking around in those shoes, if you can even walk at all.

Same with drug laws, with drugs being illegal at the federal level, the government has seen it as their right to intervene - which means the true cause never gets addressed - addiction. Addiction occurs when there is an emotional or biological need that isn't being met, and putting addicts in jail is supposed to fix this? Both assisted suicides and drug addiction are medical issues not legal ones. Prohibitions on grounds of morality have caused more trouble than fixing anything, because it takes away the autonomy of the states, the privacy between doctor and patient, and the liberty of the people to make their own choices, whether good or bad for them.

When you hear of a prostitution ring being busted on the other side of the nation - do you start thinking this country's going straight to hell? - I don't, because that's in another state, not mine. What do I care what happens in Florida, Maine or New York, I might visit but never plan on living there. We shouldn't care either, the states are sovereign and it's time they are treated that way again with the reemergence of the lost art of *Nullification*.

Nullification is a very misunderstood and maligned practice, because its critics immediately equate it with laws advancing bigotry. To be fair there have been times it was used for that, such as Jim Crow laws, but it has also been used to curtail it - segregation laws were federal and the states that disapproved nullified those mandates. Basically, nullification gives the states and the people the constitutional right to ignore the federal mandates that they deem as unconstitutional.

So let's take that list of prohibitions - if the residents of Oregon wanted to legalize prostitution, and three-fourths of the state said yes, then the residents of the state can ignore any federal laws prohibiting it; or if Nevada wanted to change their drug laws, so not only Medical Marijuana was legal, but all bans on it were lifted, they could nullify the Controlled Substances Act. Critics on this have said that people from other states would come just to get high - so what? If you visit a state where alcohol is illegal, do you have to stay dry when visiting someplace it's not? No, that would be absurd.

No matter what the issue is, *it's up to that state and its people* to decide their laws. We are a united country but *sovereign states* and America was never meant to be uniform in anyway. Our greatest strength lies in our differences, let's keep it that way.

Security-Liberty=Tyranny

The attitude on the right is this advocacy of proactive military actions and intervention in the everyday operations of their political and social structure, is bewildering, to me. Mostly for these two reasons:

First, the republicans and conservatives claim to espouse the principles of the founding fathers - the founders didn't push for continuous military engagements in countries with dubious validations for our involvement and with vague end results. The War on Terror, for one, went from being a valid argument of going after the perpetrators of the attacks on the World Trade Center, to the larger agenda of ridding the world of tyrants of the Middle East. How do you eliminate the tyrants without becoming one yourself? The capacity of involvement with other nations that the founders practiced was mostly that of free trade, and only intervene in a larger capacity, if our nation's interests or the nation itself were threatened.

The second reason, it doesn't make sense - this proactive strike philosophy was advanced by Woodrow Wilson, a progressive Democrat. Prior to World War I we only had one or two wars we entered under disputable intentions - after it we entered into wars because the other nation's leaders looked at us wrong.

The only thing more convoluted than the right's push to go to war, is the left's push against going to war - saying they don't want war, but going to war anyways. All this is part of a larger mentality that if you give up control of what's going on in the world; all chaos will be the result. If the government

224

stops spying on its *own* citizens, it won't know if they are spies. Isn't this pretty much a modern version of *McCarthyism*? It is important to stay alert, but security is not worth it if you can't employ a policy that respects our rights of privacy, there is a way to do it, but this isn't it.

Time for some Housecleaning

Actually we're been too long for a housecleaning and senate cleaning as well, get rid of the ones who aren't looking out for the good of their constituency and replace them with fresh faces. They are your representatives and don't let them forget that; if they ask for increases in taxes, ask them how they are going to spend it; if they ask for a new building project, ask its purpose; and if you don't like their answers tell them to pack their bags.

On the list of those who have violated their oaths – Congresswoman Maxine Waters, Congressman Charlie Rangel, Senator Joe Manchin, Senator Chuck Schumer, Congresswoman Nancy Pelosi, Senator John McCain, Senator Lindsey Graham, Senator Harry Reid, Senator Patrick Leahy, Congresswoman Sheila Lee Jackson, Senator Dick Durbin, Senator Orrin Hatch, Senator Elizabeth Warren, Senator Barbara Boxer, Senator Al Franken, Senator Max Baucus and Congressman Eric Cantor.

Attitude Means a Lot

One of the easiest solutions to the problems of our nation is, sadly, also probably the most difficult to achieve. It's the simplest thing that we could do and is the most definitive trait of a truly civilized society, and that is to listen. Listening to others is the key to understanding others; listening is how we show respect to others, which is the key the reason for all this division - people thinking others aren't listening to them. It's safe to say that is the case for most of us at least.

We are so eager to get our opinions known, that we rudely interrupt others and mock them for their views without hearing their reasoning for their conclusions. Maybe they have a point; maybe they have a solution to a problem you never considered; maybe from their life experiences they've gained knowledge you don't have. At the very least, by listening to them, maybe they will listen to you, here's an example: In Steven Schussler's book *It's a Jungle In There*, he discusses the lessons he learned in setting up his Rainforest Cafes as well as other restaurants, in one of the stories he had an encounter with PETA. To try to appeal to the group he joined the organization and invited them into the café to talk and enjoy a meal, now, Schussler was in the right here; he gave the group respect and listened to their objections; PETA, was very wrong, the group formed an opinion and didn't care to hear Schussler out.

226

Individuals and organizations do this all the time, close themselves off from others and decide before hand - in other words, they're right and you're wrong.

The real meaning of the word compromise has been turned on its head and is now referring to a complete caving in. In debates, what is needed is to have real open debates, in which all opinions are heard and discussed. After hearing it, if it doesn't make sense, it's a dishonest argument or illogical analysis, at least you heard them out. If nothing else it gives you a chance to hone your arguments, so you can always learn from the experience.

Respecting the Public Trust... Funds

Another change is attitude that needs to become a reality, is not only that of respect of others opinions, but how their money is being spent. There are a lot of pet projects that tax dollars are being spent on, that shouldn't be, such as; the *Endowments for the Arts* and NPR, in the *Affordable Care Act*, 115,000 abortions will be covered using tax dollars - it doesn't matter if your pro-choice or pro-life - you're paying for a service that doesn't help you, or the "general welfare." Your tax dollars paid to have the White House remodeled numerous times, even when the people's house was closed for tours during the government shutdown.

Your tax dollars pay for the maintenance of public services such as, libraries and parks - even if not properly maintained; same as roads and infrastructure projects in states you don't live in, and might not actually even need repair, but the states have to spend the federal money, or lose it.

One of the biggest scams in the federal budget is our foreign aid policy, basically we borrow money to meet our obligations and turn around and give part of it to other countries, in an effort to force them into accepting our nation's philosophies - this is neither, practical or moral.

We have 50% of American Citizens on some form of government assistance, with far too many on SNAP and unemployment. This system of dependency should never have started to begin with, but at this point it's not going to be sustainable for much longer. My suggestion for this is simple: First, do an across the board cut to *all* federal programs of 5-10% the first year, along with an audit for abuse and inefficiencies, making sure it's all being broadcast on TV and the internet, then cut the programs that are a drain on the economy; then the next year, cut 15-20%, and keep cutting until we get down to a 10% flat tax.

The cause of this attitude of acceptance for mismanagement of general funds, is due to the fact that since the government doesn't see your money as your's, but as a loan, it's acceptable to spend it how they see fit - if you, like me, think that your money belongs to you, than let them know this spending is unacceptable.

Go Private First

This is another scary prospect for the general public, making their favorite social institutions of the country privatized - in their psyche, imagery of total anarchy ensues. The public envisions; corporations taking over, prices skyrocketing, unsanitary and unsafe conditions and foreign investors calling the shots in America.

Maybe they're right, maybe all those things could happen with everything being done by the private sector, but there's a problem in their analysis they forgot - all those concerns are already infecting the system in the public sector. Corporations foreign and domestic have enormous influence in *all* industries already, but the costs of business and workplace conditions are improved in private companies. Why? - Corporations are greedy and only care about the bottom line? They don't care about the workers, do they? Or about their customers?

Actually, they do care and it's because *of* the profit motivation - the presidents of the companies have to offer competitive benefits and wages to find the best workers, plus having to pay for training new employees isn't cheap. As for their customers, I know firsthand that corporations will bend over backwards for their customers; they want to maintain a positive public image and avoid bad word of mouth.

The most important way that the private sector is an improvement is that in order to keep customers, they have to constantly upgrade features of their goods and services. The public sector doesn't have to make a better TV set, computer or phone. The public sector doesn't have to create better features to their systems and services. All the concerns that the public has with the private sector rarely happen, because the public demands more. Monopolies don't happen with private companies, since when they do the general public raises hell, but when these inefficiencies occur in the public sector, unions, special interests and the sleeping media covers it up.

All we really need to be run by the government is the courts, and that's to make sure that people aren't being taken advantage of. Parks, schools, libraries, hospitals, safety interests, all have been run into repair in government hands; so let's give the private sector a chance, they have a better track record.

Remember it won't be easy, But it will be worth it

In Michael Moore's film *Sicko*, one of the examples he uses as a model for Universal Healthcare is the country of Norway and the efforts by their Progress Party - this liberal parliamentary party, got them to economic solvency. They have a single-payer healthcare system now, which Moore likes, but what he neglects to tell you is how they got there.

In 1969, when Phillips Petro Co. discovered petroleum at the Eskofisk field, the country started using the money from the company to pay off their debts and investing in a Sovereign Wealth fund, similar to the way the industrialists did during the industrial revolution in America. Before our country started borrowing from other countries, the government would borrow from the industrialists, the government still gets money from big business but for the most part it's under the table.

But back to Norway, the Phillips Petro Co. didn't show a net profit until the 1980's and endured a depression until then, the way the country got its Universal Healthcare system was they utilized practical economic discipline and enduring through hard times, *not* from borrowing from other nations. Borrowing is the modern American way of running the government checkbook and while I don't suggest starting a Universal Healthcare system, the basic principles are the same tools to achieving economic freedom - tax cuts and economic liberalization, the same practical economics that capitalists use.

That was a pretty convenient fact for Moore to leave out, that Norway using capitalist principles to achieve a socialist end. Those long forgotten economic tools needs to be brought back - live within a budget, don't borrow and don't start social programs without a plan to reach self-sufficiency. Politicians argue that finances for the government are different from the individual, it is different, and it's *more* important to be frugal, because the public is putting the trust in your decisions. To return to economic freedom won't be easy, it will require a lot of sacrifice, more by some than others; but in the end it will be worth it.

Skepticism Revival

Skepticism is the key that has been missing in discussions, but not the regular run-of-the-mill skepticism - which tells us that things like, ghosts, aliens or sasquatch aren't real, but open skepticism - the kind that entertains the notion that such things *could* exist. It's frankly the only pragmatic way of analyzing information - because as the conspiracy theorists have shown, there is truth behind the myths. There is physical evidence to suggest unusual, unknown creatures might be out there, whether it is the before mentioned or not, something is out there. The government of Canada thinks Sasquatch exists; they declared it an endangered species. Ghost hunters have presented atmospheric anomalies in the areas of hauntings. Alien encounters victims have suffered reports of time loss.

Does all this mean that we are surrounded by beings of myths, folklore and fairy tales - maybe, maybe not, but skeptics and nonbelievers take their singular opinion and go with it. One of the claims by skeptics is that all the people reporting these encounters are less educated or poverty stricken, who have seen an unidentified creature and misidentified it - that's not only extremely patronizing, but not at all true. Sightings have spread throughout all social classes, with varying educations. There are other possible explanations for the phenomena, but to dismiss the claims outright without properly investigating the matter is not only lazy, but dishonest - groups like, the illuminati really do exist, there really is fluoride in the drinking water and there is possibility of the earth getting hit by a rouge planet like the theory of Nibiru suggests.

But the other major institutions of society are not being properly vetted as conspiracy theories are; the virtuous absolutists don't question theological institutions, and emotional absolutists don't question humanitarian institutions and neither question the motives of those involved. The best way to operate is to listen to both the proponents and the critics in issues, this doesn't violate religious or humanitarian principles, since it's questioning the people who created them, about their inefficiencies and their motives - in other words, *critical analysis of our social institutions is not an on assault on them, but proper vetting of the people involved.* All human institutions should be questioned: religion, science, government, social programs, and humanitarians; when viewing everything with as much a possibility of it being wrong as right is how you find the truth.

Restoring True Hope

Things look bleak, I know, we can't trust our own institutions, most have either failed us or swindled us. The government takes your money, trust and freedoms; they ignore public objections to laws that don't protect us, and do all they can to enslave us using our own economic infrastructure. Some religions and their leaders have done the same; we have cults - that abuse their followers trust, racial supremacy and bigotry, all in the name of God.

Humanitarians such as groups like PETA, ELF and Planned Parenthood, talk down to us or scream at us for being evil, because we disagree with them. We have technology that the leaders of not only our country, but all nations, have abused by their "gracious" and benevolent leaders. So, how can we possibly dare to hope that things will improve?

For one thing this is nothing new; it has happened in pretty much every country at one time or another. Think about the fall of the Soviet Union, things are better in many parts of the former Russian Federation. They got through it and so will the United States. Mostly, it's because we - the general public - know what is going on, that is revolutionary. We know the problems and the ways, in which our leaders operate, thanks to the modern information technology, we can only be caged up so much.

Russia is going through a major social and political change because of this technology as well, the Russians know the true history of their country thanks to the internet and Putin has had the smallest victory yet and there is a growing rise in opposition of him. We know what is going on in the Middle East and other dictatorial regimes, thanks to the internet, we know all this and across the planet people are waking up.

Even former Obama supporters see him as a tyrant; the NSA spying has brought inquiries about the data mining violations, by many of the Hollywood elite, being led by Oliver Stone.

Amongst the general public the president's approval rating is in the negative 39% to 54%, with the damage of the *Affordable Care Act*. We know what is happening and it scares us, but it's great that we know. We didn't know what many of the earlier presidents were *really* doing - we didn't know what Woodrow Wilson was doing, or Theodore Roosevelt or Franklin Roosevelt. With knowledge we can get off the road to serfdom and back to on the expressway to opportunity.

So What is Unconventional Wisdom?

So, what is UnConventional Wisdom? It's finding a practical solution to problems that works within economic and ethical principles. A solution that is without emotional blackmail, that doesn't encourage the usage of laws to cut back moral decay - because a law is force, and a forced morality doesn't work. *UnConventional Wisdom* also means that those who are prosperous can keep the fruits of their labor, whether they have $200 or $200,000,000, they know how to spend it better than anybody else - any other solutions are also in fact, immoral and inhumane. So, let's see if you can now think using the *UnConventional Wisdom* solutions in these hypothetical scenarios:

First example: You're a police officer and you have brought in a suspect for questioning in a spree of murders. How do you proceed? The Conventional Wisdom is to go in there and do whatever it takes to

235

get a confession, even if it takes all night and you have to lie or feed him details of the case. After all you know in your gut he did it. There's a problem here, these tactics also lead to a high number of false arrests and are unethical.

Now, to do this the UnConventional Wisdom way - You can't lie to the suspect, that's unethical and a law enforcer who will bend one set of ethics is more likely to bend others. In short if it's illegal for you to lie to the police, it should be illegal for them to lie to you. That means the officer has to change tactics, that's all, but human psychology is on their side - studies have shown that being honest to the suspects gets them to confess too.

My theory on this; with the case of passion killers, their guilt betrays them, let them know they are your main suspect, show them photos of the crime and release them to stew in their guilt. Check back in a couple of weeks and press them again. Sooner or later they will confess. But if we're dealing with a hardened sociopath here, that won't work since they don't feel guilt, but they do feel pride. Tell them how impressive the crime was and ask them if they think there was a trophy what it is, killers are some of the biggest narcissists out there and will tell you everything.

Second example: At the scene of a bombing, the suspect was also killed; in the list of the dead is a pregnant woman, a Muslim, a man with a displayed confederate flag tattoo on his arm, an old lady and Goth teenager with a Marilyn Manson T-shirt on.

Who bombed the building? The initial response, depending on ideology, would be either the Muslim or the racist, after that the Goth teen. But let's look again using UnConventional Wisdom, and the placement of the bodies tells the whole story.

The Muslim had jumped in front of the pregnant woman futilely shielding her, so he didn't do it. He's also not a Muslim, but an Italian; he just has a dark complexion. So, how about the racist he loves guns and explosions, and wanted to kill that dirty Muslim, that would be hard to do when you're running for the door. He's not a hero, but he's not a killer, and the Goth was right behind him. It was the old lady, the last suspect, but why? Well, it has to do with the building, it's an insurance office and after years of faithfully paying her premiums on time - her policy was canceled, and she is going to die from a terminal illness.

Last example: In a retail store there is a robbery and shooting that is moments away from occurring, will it be the grungy man with the AR-15 on his back and the glocks strapped to his thighs, or the man in the suit, who might have concealed pistols under his suit coat? Let's just say that the hypothetical incident could have been prevented if security hadn't asked the first guy to leave. While security was escorting him out the second pulled out his guns and killed the first guy and the security guards, before going on a shooting spree inside.

Acting on preconceived notions about others is not only a

ridiculous practice, but at times dangerous. But that's not where *UnConventional Wisdom* ends; it's also about protecting the weakest. Like against politicians that are under the impression they have authority to side-step state laws; or take citizens property using *eminent domain*; or force people to buy services they don't need or want; or make your decisions on what you do to with, or put in, or on your body - if they can make those choices for you, what else can they decide for you?

Using *UnConventional Wisdom*, we can come up with the solutions to all those issues, and these are some of the tools: nullification, stopping reactionary policies, respect the constitution, avoid prohibition laws, empower the third parties, introduce choices, encourage self-sufficiency and the most important of all - stay vigilant. Pay attention to what your leaders are doing, and make sure their policies are for your good and not theirs. So, what is *UnConventional Wisdom*? - It's commonsense, practical actions using logical analysis to satisfy *legal* principles, free from any sort of bias.

Final Thoughts: Pavlov got it wrong

The biggest error that the *Pavlovian Social Engineers* are making, is the same one that Pavlov himself made, they misunderstood their subject of study. Dogs are smart, emotional beings that have a higher understanding of humans than we do of them. Did you know that wolves don't bark? - That's an action that dogs developed, the speculation of why they developed it is so they could communicate with us. Pavlov thought that dogs were a lesser species and treated them as such. This is the same thing the *Pavlovian Social Engineers* - Barack Obama, Woodrow Wilson, Theodore Roosevelt, Franklin Roosevelt, and the key figures in their administrations - do as well; this is more commonly known as *Social Darwinism.*

The theory is that since there are certain individuals that are born with biological advantages - higher intellect, better social status, or whatever superficial criteria the establishment declare worthy - they have the moral authority to act for the masses. This is actually a reversal of social evolution, because those in power are trying to implement a more tribal hierarchal social structure; rather than the civilized one, where the individual is left to make their own decisions. If they were really the more advanced they would realize that fact, and gladly abdicate this perceived "right" to make others decisions.

We as individuals need to figure out what is best for us; whether it's healthcare, personal morals, economics or political ideology - and fight to be left alone, otherwise like Pavlov's dogs, we could end up drooling at the sound of the government's bell.

Speech is given to many; intelligence to few.

Special Thanks

First **and foremost I** would have to thank my parents - not only for their moral (and at times, financial) support, but for the manner they raised me. I learned from you about hard work and *real* fair play - that the only true equality is the one that has the same rules for all. Love you guys. Thanks also to my brother, for being there and buying the first copy of *'We the Rodents'*, also thanks to my sister for her moral support. Thanks to my extended family, my nieces and nephews, and my Aunts and Uncles and their families, for the life's lessons I learned from you.

Thanks to my former roommate, John, for the crazy conversations, oh by the way have you heard from sasquatch? I kind of miss him. Thanks to Jimmy, for your friendship and the madness that ensued from only a couple hours of sleep and a *Monster* energy drink, on those early mornings at work. Thanks to Erica Jo, and my most dear friend Stephanie, for your input on social issues. Thanks to the "Three Wise men of Social Issues," Larry, Paul and Rick.

Thanks to the staff of the *Washington Times, Wall Street Journal,* and *Reason Magazine.* Especially, Jessica Chasmir of the *Washington Times,* for keeping me in the know. Thanks to the journalists and commentators - John Stossel, Bernard Goldberg, Greg Gutfield, Neal Boortz, Glenn Beck, Thomas

Woods Jr., and Judge Andrew Napolitano. I also would like to thank the contributing writers and the editing staff, of the *Opposing Viewpoints* book series.

Thanks to the few politicians that I believe in, Dr. Ron Paul, his son Rand Paul, Ted Cruz, Mike Lee, Justin Amash, Gary Johnson, Dr. Ben Carson, Thomas Massie, and any other politician who understands voluntarism and the principles of our constitution. Thanks also to the authors of the *Federalist Papers*, the *Anti-Federalist Papers*, the *Declaration of Independence*, the *United States Constitution* and the *Virginia Resolutions*, with special recognition to Thomas Jefferson and James Madison. Lastly, I would have to thank the American people, for finally waking up.

References **and recommended Reading**

All the books listed in the following have had an impact on me and my perception and the journey to this point, to not list them would be, well, sacrilege. I hope you find the authors as insightful and entertaining as I did.

America in Danger	Stephen M. Studdert
Arrogant	Bernard Goldberg
Bias	Bernard Goldberg
Candide	Voltaire
Do As I Say (Not As I Do)	Peter Scheizer
First Principles	John B. Taylor
Freakonomics	Steven D. Leavitt Stephen J. Dubner
Freedom: For The Thought We Hate	Anthony Lewis
Give Me a Break	John Stossel
Give Us Liberty: A Tea Party Manifesto	Dick Armey Matt Kibbe
Homeland Insecurity	Terry D. Turchie Kathleen M. Puckett, PhD
Joy of Hate	Greg Gutfield
Mad as Hell	Doug Schoen Scott Rasmussen

244

About the Author

R. C. Seely started the *Americanus Libertae* movement in the winter 2012. It started with a blog at Wordpress.com with that name. That same year he wrote the book *'We the Rodents.'* He started MOJO Publishing at that time and a YouTube channel. Prior to this book, in the same year, he also wrote *LEGACY.*

He continues the efforts of *Americanus Libertae* of exposing the dangers in Pop Culture and advancing the third parties.

He can be reached at *americanuslibertae@gmail.com* and releases updates at *RCSeely@AmLibertae.twitter.com.*